THE EGO
IS NOT THE
REAL YOU

ALSO BY DAVID R. HAWKINS, M.D., Ph.D.

Books

Power vs. Force: The Hidden Determinants of Human Behavior

The Eye of the I: From Which Nothing Is Hidden

I: Reality and Subjectivity

Truth vs. Falsehood: How to Tell the Difference

Transcending the Levels of Consciousness: The Stairway to Enlightenment

Discovery of the Presence of God: Devotional Nonduality

Reality, Spirituality and Modern Man

Healing and Recovery

Along the Path to Enlightenment

Dissolving the Ego, Realizing the Self

Letting Go: The Pathway of Surrender

Success Is for You: Using Heart-Centered Principles for Lasting Abundance and Fulfillment

Book of Slides: The Complete Collection Presented at the 2002–2011 Lectures with Clarifications

The Map of Consciousness Explained: A Proven Energy Scale to Actualize Your Ultimate Potential

Audio Programs

The Map of Consciousness Explained

How to Surrender to God

Live Life as a Prayer

Please visit:

Hay House USA: www.hayhouse.com®
Hay House Australia: www.hayhouse.com.au
Hay House UK: www.hayhouse.co.uk
Hay House India: www.hayhouse.co.in

THE EGO
IS NOT THE
REAL YOU

Wisdom to
Transcend the Mind
and Realize the Self

DAVID R. HAWKINS,
M.D., Ph.D.

HAY HOUSE, INC.
Carlsbad, California • New York City
London • Sydney • New Delhi

Published in the United States by: Hay House, Inc.: www.hayhouse
.com® • **Published in Australia by:** Hay House Australia Pty. Ltd.:
www.hayhouse.com.au • **Published in the United Kingdom by:**
Hay House UK, Ltd.: www.hayhouse.co.uk • **Published in India
by:** Hay House Publishers India: www.hayhouse.co.in

Cover design: Julie Davison • *Interior design:* Nick C. Welch

**Cataloging-in-Publication Data is on file at the Library
of Congress**

Tradepaper ISBN: 978-1-4019-6423-8
E-book ISBN: 978-1-4019-6424-5

11 10 9 8 7 6 5 4 3 2
1st edition, August 2021

Printed in the United States of America

This product uses papers sourced from responsibly managed
forests. For more information, see www.hayhouse.com.

Gloria in Excelsis Deo!

CONTENTS

Introduction   1

PART I: The Nature of the self (Ego/Mind)   7

PART II: Surrendering the Self   49

PART III: The Divinity of the Self   77

Glossary   141
Bibliography   149
About the Author   151

Note: References to the Map of Consciousness and the concept of calibration are explained in detail in Dr. Hawkins's book *Power vs. Force*.

INTRODUCTION

"Spiritual processing is like positioning oneself in the wind."

— DAVID R. HAWKINS, M.D., PH.D.

Have you ever seen a tree in autumn with half its leaves gone and then a powerful gust of wind blows through and all the remaining leaves drop instantly to the ground? This book can be that powerful wind for you. Like the tree that's already dropped many of its leaves, you are ready to let go of a lot of old ways of thinking and limiting patterns of anxiety, grief, guilt, shame, and anger.

Let this book be the force that clears away the rest of the "leaves" that you're hanging on to without even realizing they're there—the false promises of the ego, those hard-to-see attachments and false beliefs that prevent you from realizing that you are one with All. As we know by watching the seasons, a tree has to go through the winter's letting go before it can yield the springtime's blossoms.

Are you willing to let go of seeing yourself as the ego believes you to be? Are you willing to go further, to know that the ego *itself* is an illusion? Dr. Hawkins tells us that even the idea of the separate self as a seeker of Truth is an illusion: "It is a hindrance to consider that there is a personal self or an 'I' or an ego that is doing the striving or seeking, or that will become enlightened. It is much easier to realize there is no such thing as the ego or an 'I' identity that is doing any seeking; instead, it is an impersonal aspect of consciousness that is doing the exploring and seeking."

This process is a shift from "who" we are to "what" we are. I learned this from Dr. Hawkins in a funny way. One day he made up a nickname for me, "Fran-Fran," and this instigated a series of knock-knock jokes between us:

Doc: Fran-Fran.

Fran: Doc-Doc.

Doc: Knock-knock.

Fran: Who's there?

Doc: It's not a "who" but a "what."

We then broke into laughter. Do you see how brilliant he was at using humor to crack open old habits of perception? Even as he connected to me as a person, a "who," his humor cut through the illusion of personhood. He said, "You are not a 'who' but a 'what.'" The ego personality is fixated on being a successful "who" in the world, such as "I am this . . . I've done that . . . I own this . . . I believe in that . . ." Dr. Hawkins recommends that, instead of focusing on "who" we are, we ask ourselves in continual contemplation, "*What* am I?"

As we surrender "who" we think we are, we come to the "what," the Source of existence itself. Letting go of identities and personas, beliefs and attachments, and even letting go of ourselves as seekers, what is left?

I remember a moment when I was with him and it dawned on me: "I'm not a professor, though I work as one. I'm not a devotee, though I serve as one. I'm not a woman, though I live as one. I'm not a 'me,' though I function as one." The "what" replaces "who." Love dissolves every "who" we try to hang on to. The river loses its name when it flows into the sea.

In this book, key teachings from Dr. Hawkins's body of work have been selected to guide us in this process of Self-realization. Any one of the teachings,

THE EGO IS NOT THE REAL YOU

if applied directly, reveals the Truth. "Any leg of the elephant leads to the elephant," as Dr. Hawkins says.

As we read the book, Dr. Hawkins recommends that we seek to "know" rather than "know about." "Know" implies subjective experience; "know about" means to accumulate facts.

And he also recommends this inner prayer:

> Ask to be the servant of the Lord, a vehicle of Divine Love, a channel of God's Will. Ask for direction and divine assistance and surrender all personal will through devotion. Dedicate one's life to the service of God. Choose love and peace above all other options. Commit to the goal of unconditional love and compassion for all life in all its expressions and surrender all judgment to God. — *The Eye of the I: From Which Nothing Is Hidden* (2002), Chapter 13: Explanations, p. 265.

If we can give up the illusion of this little "me," Dr. Hawkins promises that unsurpassable joy will be ours: "There is absolutely nothing in ordinary human experience to compare with the joy of the Presence of the Love of God. No sacrifice is too great nor effort too much in order to realize that Presence." He verifies this promise with the certitude that's possible *only* from having, himself, surrendered everything on the altar of the Ultimate.

This book is small in size, but it can have a massive impact on your life. It will take you through the process of a total transformation of consciousness—if you choose to apply its teachings deeply within yourself.

With devotion and gratitude,
Fran Grace, Ph.D.

PART I

THE NATURE
OF THE
SELF
(EGO/MIND)

While the mind secretly believes that its survival is due to the ego, on the contrary, the person's survival is due to the spirit that energizes the ego to accomplish important tasks. It is because of the intention of the spirit that the lower self or ego even remembers to take its vitamins. In truth, we exist and survive, not because of the ego, but in spite of it.

∽✦∾

The world of the ego is like a house of mirrors through which the ego wanders, lost and confused, as it chases the images in one mirror after another. Human life is characterized by endless trials and errors while attempting to escape the maze. At times, for many people—and possibly for most—the world of mirrors becomes a house of horrors that gets worse and worse. The only way out of the circuitous wanderings is through the pursuit of spiritual truth.

∽✦∾

It is important to remember that the world operates within the limited Newtonian paradigm of linear causality which has its prevailing perceptions of what is "real." Spirituality, on the other hand, is based on the invisible realities and realms of nonduality and therefore may seem unreal or, at best, an oddity to the ordinary world.

❧

Everything is happening of its own; nothing is causing anything else. . . . It is critical to grasp that the illusion of linear causality as an explanation for the observed phenomena of life is the major and most profound limitation of thinkingness. . . . Mentation, reason, logic, and language are all structured dualistically, based on the axiom that there is a subject and an object, that there is a "this" doing or causing a "that."

❧

That the human mind, without help, is unable to tell truth from falsehood due to its own innate structure and design is so staggering a discovery that it is roughly comparable to the discovery by Copernicus that caused cultural shock in the 16th century. Because this single fact alone is confrontational to the average mind, it will probably not be welcomed or warmly greeted by those who profit from sophistry and its illusions.

❧

Profound silence is more influential and beneficial than an avalanche of redundant words and actions that emanate from the spiritual ego and its platitudinous rationalizations. Spiritual rhetoric is still just rhetoric and represents spiritual sophistry. Commitment to enlightenment alters and recontextualizes social roles.

∾

The mind acts as a processor of data simultaneously from both within and without. . . . Some of the information is perceived and stored in memory banks, but there is also unconscious processing of all the data that is stored in the unconscious. This processing screening device results in the 1/10,000th of a second's delay and acts as a separation between self and Self/Reality. This processing screen represents "the experiencer" in action.

∾

The experiencer screen is energized by desire and identification with it. This desire is like an appetite of curiosity, wantingness, and craving, and is an addiction to the experience of experiencing itself. In addition, there is identification with experiencing and its content information as "self."

∾

Energy fields are so powerful that they dominate our perception. They are really portals out of which we see the world. We often hear that this is really just a world of mirrors, and that all we experience is our own energy field reflected back upon us as perception and experiencing.

∞

The ego can be thought of as a set of entrenched habits of thought, which are the results of entrainment by invisible energy fields that dominate human consciousness. They become reinforced by repetition and by the consensus of society. Further reinforcement comes from language itself. To think in language is a form of self-programming. The use of the pronoun *I* as the subject—and therefore the implied cause of all actions—is the most serious error, and automatically creates a duality of subject and object.

∞

From a greater context, we can view that the ego is not "evil" but is primarily a self-interested animal. Unless the "animal self" is understood and accepted, its influence cannot be diminished.

∞

It is clear that the instinctual origins of the ego mechanisms are based on satisfaction and gratification of survival needs and desires.

∽

The narcissistic core of the ego is aligned with being "right," whether being "right" means being in agreement with wisdom or rejecting it as invalid. With humility, the serious searcher discovers that the mind alone, despite its education, is unable to resolve the dilemma of how to ascertain and validate truth—which would require confirmation by subjective experience as well as objective, provable criteria.

∽

It is most important to remember that to violate principle for practical expediency is to relinquish enormous power. The rationalization that the execution of criminals deters crime, for instance, does not hold up under study; and the end does not justify the means. . . . Because we fail to differentiate principle from expediency, the average person lacks the discernment to understand the difference between patriotism and true Patriotism, between americanism and Americanism, between god and God, between freedom and Freedom, between liberty and Liberty.

Thus, "americanism" is used as a justification by white supremacy groups (calibrated at 150) and lynch mobs, just as warmongering throughout history has been conducted in the name of "God." . . . Learning the difference between principles and their imitators requires experience and educated judgment. The exercise of such discretion is necessary for moral survival in the modern world in general but is imperative in those gray areas where ethical ambiguity has been elevated from convention to an art form: the political arena and the marketplace of daily commerce.

∽

Radical truth means what is being experienced, not what one is actually thinking about it or the concepts that one is projecting onto the experience; it is not the labeling of it but what one is literally experiencing within oneself.

∽

The brain is the sense organ of the experiencer, and one realizes that it is destined for physical death. Therefore, the importance of the Self rather than the self is realized by accepting the inevitability of mortality.

∽

Concepts have levels of power that can be calibrated. The higher the level of truth, the greater its power. The energy of the concept results from the truth of the statement plus the level of consciousness of the speaker. Unaided by a higher energy (as from a great teacher), the ego/mind cannot transcend itself.

∽

Opposites do not exist in Reality. They are only concepts of speech and mentation. Let us take the seeming opposites of light and dark. Actually, there is no such thing as darkness; there is only light. The conditions then can be accurately described as light is either present or not, or light is present at various degrees; therefore, all light or the lack of it can be defined only in terms of light by its presence or degree, or not. Thus, there is only *one variable*: the presence or absence of light.

∽

A verbalization helps to set a context that then progressively becomes nonverbal and more inclusive. Accurate information saves time and speeds fruitful inquiry by indicating which routes would be fruitlessly time-consuming and diversionary.

∽

If time is nonexistent, then so is the notion of "place." . . . "Space" is a concept. The mind imagines that if something exists in a place, then that place must be a space. Like time, "space" is an imagination. . . . In the nonlinear Reality, there is no time track upon which to position a moment or an instant denotable as "now."

∽∾

The study of form is fascinating to the intellect in its expressions of physics, chemistry, astronomy, cosmology, etc. Man then begins to ask where the universe came from and where is it going. Actually, this demonstrates another animal instinct that is very important, that of curiosity. In order to find food, a mate, or shelter, the animal is always instinctively searching and seems to have an insatiable curiosity. Exploration is innate to mankind, and its highest levels lead to spiritual inquiry. This brings up the questions of who am I, what am I, where did I come from, what is the origin and destiny of the self, and who and where is God.

∽∾

All aspects of human life are transient; therefore, to cling to any aspect eventually brings grief and loss.

Each incident, however, is an opportunity to search within for the source of life, which is ever present, unchanging, and not subject to loss or the ravages of time.

∽✺∾

The body itself is actually not experienced; instead, only the *sensations* of the body are experienced. Therefore, awareness of the body is merely a composite sensation by which the somatic area of the brain records input, and, by neuronal function, replicates the body image.

∽✺∾

Ultimately, everything is knowable only by virtue of the identity of "being it." The conundrums of epistemology can be solved only by the elimination of thought because all languaging is a paradox. One can take any word and trace it to its roots. How does the word originate? From where? Is the word the same thing as its meaning? By asking such questions, one is eventually confronted with the ultimate paradox of duality. The radical Reality is that to understand the essence of anything is to know God. One might say that all languaging is a substitute for God.

∽✺∾

There is no timetable or prescribed route to God. Although each person's path is unique, the terrain to be covered is relatively common to all. The work is to surmount and transcend the common human failings that are inherent in the structure of the human ego. One would like to think that these failings are personal; however, the ego itself is not personal. It was inherited along with becoming a human being. Details differ based on past karma.

∽◊∾

That "it" of the ego structure is not unique or individual, and it is relatively similar, with karmic variations, in everyone. What really varies from individual to individual is the degree to which one is enslaved by its programs. The degree of dominance is therefore determined by the extent to which one identifies with it. Inherently, it has no power, and the power to decline the ego's programs increases exponentially as one progresses spiritually.

∽◊∾

Because of its inherent limitations, the ego itself cannot know God experientially. God is the absolute subjectivity that underlies existence and the capacity for awareness. God is beyond all time, place, or human characteristics. All the descriptions of the Ultimate Reality by enlightened beings throughout history have been identical. There is only one Supreme Reality. . . . Inasmuch as the Godhead, or God Unmanifest, is beyond all depiction, the Ultimate Realization is radically and purely subjective and absent of all content. To acknowledge the absolute divinity of the Infinite Supreme would be unacceptable to entities that are deluded into claiming godship. We can then say that a false deity is an entity that has declined truth for power, pride, and control over others, and has succumbed to the Luciferic error which proclaims that the ego is God (i.e., megalomania). The basis for the error is the unwillingness to surrender sovereignty from the "I" of the ego to the Allness of God.

∽✺∾

Pride in the form of the vanity of thought, mentation, concepts, and opinions is the basis of ignorance. The antidote is radical humility, which undoes the domination of perception. . . . To enter the domain of reality is like going through a fine screen—only clear water can traverse through it, and all the fish, bugs, and debris are left outside. Only pure consciousness devoid of content can pass through the barriers of perception and become the clear water beyond the screen. . . . The finite is born of the infinite and is never actually separated from it except by perception; the infinite potentiality of the unmanifest becomes the actuality of the manifest by the will of God as Creation.

∽

Traditionally, the readiness for spiritual learning has been termed "ripeness," indicating a fortuitous combination of sincere intention plus maturity, progressive evolution of consciousness, and activation of the desire for experiential learning. . . . There develops an enthusiasm and eventually a dedication, and spiritual goals and values progressively replace the lesser ones of the worldly ego. . . . Progress is best described as the unfolding of realizations and spontaneous revelation that are often ascribed to intuition and inner guidance. . . . As spiritual work advances, the self progressively dissolves and merges into the Self, which has its own learning capacities that differ from those of the ego/mind.

∽

The more advanced seeker has heard that there is no "out there" or "in here" and thus takes responsibility for all that happens. There is the dawning awareness that all which seems to occur really represents what is being held in what was previously considered as "within." Thus, the proclivity to project is undone. The "innocent victim" positionality, with all its spurious "innocence," is unmasked. . . . Beliefs are the determinant of what one experiences. There are no external "causes." One discovers the secret payoffs that are obtained from unconscious secret projections. One's underlying programs can be discovered by simply writing down one's litany of grievances and woes and then merely turning them around into their opposites.

∽◊∽

The mind's reality is a fiction. With that realization, it loses its reign as the arbiter of reality. Through the eye of the ego, life is a kaleidoscope of constantly changing attractions and repulsions, fears and transient pleasures. It bases its security on overvalued positionalities, but, with maturity, it progressively looks within for enduring qualities that can be relied upon. Without spiritual direction or information, it does not know which way to look and may merely settle back into basic survival techniques that have had pragmatic value.

∽◊∽

It is well to keep in mind at all times that the ego/ mind does not experience the world but only its own perception of it.

∞♾∞

The ego is the imaginary doer behind thought and action. Its presence is firmly believed to be neces- sary and essential for survival. The reason is that the ego's primary quality is perception, and as such, it is limited by the paradigm of supposed causality.

∞♾∞

Whereas the goal of the ego/mind is primarily to do, act, acquire, or perform, the intention of con- templation is to "become." While the intellect wants to know "about," contemplation seeks Knowingness itself and autonomous wisdom. Rational thinking is time related, sequential, and linear, whereas con- templation occurs outside of sequential time. It is nonlinear and related to comprehension of essence. Devotional contemplation is a way or style of being in the world whereby one's life becomes a prayer.

∞♾∞

The ego's addiction and survival are based on the secret pleasure of negativity, which cannot be abandoned until it is first recognized, identified, and owned without shame or guilt. One has to see that this is just how the ego—which everyone inherits —operates, and recognize that it is not really personal at all.

∽✧∾

The ego secretly "loves" and clings to the position of victimhood and extracts a distorted pleasure and grim justification from pain and suffering.

∽✧∾

The ego defends its own limitations with prideful denial, thus becoming its own victim.

∽✧∾

Intrinsic to the very basic construction of the human ego is an innate innocence in that it believes in the reality or truth of its own programs and is unaware that it lacks an intrinsic capacity for self-correction. The reason for the ego's inherent lack of capacity for verification is that its data is limited to only internal processing systems. The internal mechanisms of the ego lack any external, independent source of reference for verification.

❧

As we get closer to the discovery of the source of the ego's tenacity, we make the amazing critical discovery that *we are enamored with our self.*

❧

Realization is a progressive process. Spiritual progress is hastened by understanding the true nature of the ego. It is not an enemy to be attacked or defeated, nor is it an evil to be vanquished. It is dissolved by compassionate understanding.

❧

Realistic self-esteem arises from fulfilling integrous principles so that intention becomes an important factor, which in itself is less vulnerable than idealized results. . . . It takes courage to jettison the props of pride and, with humility, accept one's inner reality, which is of an invulnerable source. To accept the inner core of one's existence as a self-existent reality requires letting go of any definitions of self as a "who" and, instead, seeing oneself as a "what." . . . All credit for accomplishments is given to God as the Presence of the Divinity within instead of to the ego, and therefore accomplishment results in gratitude and joy rather than vulnerable pridefulness.

∽⚬∾

The universe is very cooperative. Inasmuch as the universe is not different from consciousness itself, it is happy to create whatever we wish to find "out there." The problem is with the concept of cause itself, which begs the question by presuming a time warp, a sequence, or a string of events that would make sense. If we step outside of time, there are no causes at all. We could say that the manifest world originates out of the unmanifest, but that again would be inferring a sequential causal series in time—that is, unmanifest becoming manifest. Once beyond the warp of time, with its implicit restrictions of comprehension to terms of mere sequence, there is no backwards or forwards.

∽⚬∾

Because the ego is constructed of positionalities, it has no option to be anything else except what it is. It therefore becomes an inescapable source of endless suffering and loss. Above all else, it fears the future and the specter of death itself, which is intrinsic to the ego's structure.

∽⚬∾

The ego has habitual modes of determining perception. They have to be identified first before they can be disassembled. One has to give up guilt about having an ego.

∾

In contrast to the innate arrogance of the ego, true intelligence is a quality of consciousness/awareness and is not subject to attack because its essence is nonlinear. It is, however, utilized by the ego in its expression as mind, which then becomes and subserves the ego's drive for survival. Thus, the ego really uses the mind as camouflage and becomes hidden in its clever constructions.

∾

The ego is not an enemy to be subdued but merely a compilation of unexamined habits of perception.

∾

A human being is both spirit and body; therefore, it is at all times actually existing in both the linear and the nonlinear domains.

∾

Curiously, the ego's hold is weakened by acceptance, familiarity, and compassionate understanding; in contrast, it is reinforced by self-criticism, condemnation, fear, and shame.

∾

The ego conceals, whereas awareness reveals. The answer to many defective ego positions could be subsumed in the commonly overlooked sanity of "common sense."

∾

One mechanism the ego uses to protect itself is to disown the painful data and project it onto the world and others.

∾

The ego is neither bad nor an enemy, but merely an illusion to release so that something far better can replace it.

∾

There is no such thing in reality as an ego; it is merely illusory. It is made up of a compilation of arbitrary points of view supplied by mental processing and powered by feelings and emotions. These desires represent the attachments that the Buddha spoke of as the bondage of suffering. With absolute humility, the ego dissolves. It is a collection of arbitrary mental processes that gain force only because of vanity and habit. If one lets go of the vanity of thought, it dissolves. All thought is vanity. All opinions are vanities. The pleasure of vanity is therefore the basis of the ego—unplug it and it collapses.

∽

The ego is extremely tenacious and therefore often seems to require extreme conditions before it lets go of a positionality. It often takes the collective experience of millions of people over many centuries to learn even what appears to be a simple and obvious truth—namely, that peace is better than war or love is better than hate.

∽

The ego's rigidity and resistance to correction are based on narcissistic egotism, pride, and vanity. The collective egos of whole nations bring about their downfall and destruction.

∽

The ego/mind presumes and is convinced that its perceptions and interpretations of life experiences are the "real" thing and therefore "true." It also believes by projection that other people see, think, and feel the same way—if they do not, they are mistaken and therefore wrong. Thus, perception reinforces its hold by reification and presumptions.

∼✣∽

The ego clings to emotionality, which is intimately connected with its positionalities; it pretends to think that it has no other choices. To "surrender to God" means to stop looking to the ego for solace and thrills and to discover the endless, serene joy of peace. To look within is to find the underlying, ever-present source of the illumination of the mind itself.

∼✣∽

The inflated ego is devoid of reality testing as well as amelioration by reason, logic, or rationality.

∼✣∽

Although the critical level of integrity (level 200 on the Map of Consciousness) is the very threshold of spiritual progress, one can see that due to the structure of the ego, it can be difficult to achieve. The strength of the ego is such that it can be overcome only by spiritual power.

❧

Temptation stems from within; it is merely the desire to experience the ego's payoff and satisfactions of an impulse, even if it is only a curiosity or a wanting.

❧

The satisfactions of the ego are more pleasurable and addictive than the preservation of human life, much less dignity.

❧

The ego gets a grim pleasure and satisfaction from suffering and all the levels lacking integrity: pride, anger, desire, guilt, shame, and grief. The secret pleasure of suffering is addictive. Many people devote their entire lives to it and encourage others to follow suit. To stop this mechanism, the pleasure of the payoff has to be identified and willingly surrendered to God. Out of shame, the ego blocks out conscious awareness of its machinations, especially the secretiveness of the game of "victim."

❧

The human ego likes to pretend that evil exists "out there" and seduces its hapless, innocent self into inadvertently falling into the trap of seduction. The real tempter is the ego's desire for gain—whether that be sensation, excitement, advantage, prestige, or the pleasure of controlling others.

∽◈∽

To the ego, gains lie without; to the spirit, they are internal, for the ever-present joy of existence is independent of content or form. To the spirit, a sunny day or a rainy day are the same. Awareness enjoys qualities rather than grasping at form. Thus, it can enjoy "being with," without having to own or control. Awareness is not driven by goals but instead values the capacity for equal pleasure in all circumstances.

∽◈∽

The ego is a set of programs in which reason operates through a complex, multilayered series of algorithms wherein thought follows certain decision trees that are variously weighted by past experience, indoctrination, and social forces; it is therefore not a self-created condition. The instinctual drive is attached to the programs, thereby causing physiological processes to come into play.

❧

At the higher levels, the ego is seen to be an illusion, without any innate reality. The understanding of the ego is therefore useful knowledge that is to be discarded later. To attempt to do so, however, before one can dissolve it through spiritual comprehension would lead to a fictitious stance because the mind readily incorporates all learned material and subtly tries to thrive in a new, disguised form. . . . To offset the vanity of what has been learned, one focuses instead with humility on what is yet to be learned.

❧

The ego is not the real "you"; it was inherited as part of being born a human. It basically originates from the animal world, and the evolution of consciousness happened through the primitive stages of mankind's evolution, so it could be said that to seek enlightenment is to recapitulate the history of human evolution.

❧

By commitment to inner honesty, it will become apparent that the underpinning of the ego's responses is the pleasure that is derived from them. There is an inner satisfaction that is the payoff of self-pity, anger, rage, hate, pride, guilt, fear, and so on. This inner pleasure, as morbid as it may sound, energizes and propagates all these emotions. To undo their influence, it is merely necessary to be willing to forgo and surrender these questionable inner secret pleasures to God and look only to God for joy, pleasure, and happiness.

∽∾

To undo the ego, one must be willing to abandon this payoff game, with its grandstanding of emotions and repetitive rehashing of data and stories to justify its positions. One will note that the ego milks every wrong and that it has no greater pleasure than to indulge in "righteous indignation." It just "loves" that juicy positionality that has such a great payoff.

∽∾

To the ego, abandoning the self-reward dynamic is looked upon as a loss. The ego does not trust God and thereby thinks it has only itself to turn to for sustenance, survival, and pleasure. The ego has faith in its own mechanisms and not in God. It should not be faulted for this error because it has no experiential basis for comparison. Its only way out is with faith that there is a better way. It hears a spiritual truth and begins to search for it when the mind becomes disillusioned with its own fallacies and failure to achieve happiness. It finally realizes that the grim satisfaction it squeezes out of pain is a poor substitute for joy.

∽✤∾

At its roots, the ego is the extreme of selfishness and is completely lacking in all ethical principles.

∽✤∾

The persistence of the primitive ego in man is referred to as the narcissistic core of "egotism," which, at calibration levels below 200 (the critical level of integrity), indicates the persistence of the primitiveness of self-interest, disregard for the rights of others, and seeing others as enemies and competitors rather than as allies. There is nothing deadlier than the religionized ego.

∽✤∾

The ego is not only unable to correctly assess situations that are fatal, but it even willingly sacrifices life for its own ends. The ego is therefore potentially deadly and would rather "see you dead" than admit it is wrong.

❧

The ego is a victim of itself. With rigorous intro-spection, it will be discovered that the ego is really just "running a racket" for its own fun and games and survival. The real "you" is actually the loser.

❧

The spirit evolves over great periods of temporal time, with periodic reincarnations into the spiritual workshop of earth for growth and repairs. When all the repairs have been made, earthly life loses its value, and attraction and rebirth into the human domain ceases.

❧

From a developmental analysis, which utilizes consciousness-research techniques, it appears that the human ego itself is primarily the product and continuation of the presence of the survival core of the animal evolution.

❧

While the ego/self routinely takes credit for sur-vival, its true source is the presence of Divinity as Self. It is only because of the Self that the ego is capable of being self-sustaining. It is just a recipient of life energy and not its origin, as it believes.

∽∾

The clever ego expresses its inner grandiosity by seeking to replace Divinity by declaring itself to be God (or Nero, Caesar, and so on), or claiming special Divine authority by its declaration that it is Divinely ordained and therefore authorized.

∽∾

The primary underpinning of the persistence of negativity is the ego's secret payoff from negativity ("juice"). This secret payoff is the ego's only source of energy, so it sees forgiveness, as well as compassion, as the "enemy."

∽∾

Ego positions have the characteristics of disowning responsibility and placing blame "out there." In the end, the ego's payoff is the energy by which the ego persists, because it lacks the pleasure of the input of spiritual energy. The ego's payoff is its substitute for Divinity; thus, it maintains its sovereignty and is convincing in its secret, silent belief that *it* is the source of one's life itself—that is, that *it* is God.

∾

To the ego, a "want" is interpreted as a "need" and a "have to have." Thus, its seeking can become frantic, and all caution can be thrown to the wind. Desires are thereby escalated to being desperate and demanding any sacrifice, including even the deaths of *millions* of other people. It *must* have what it wants at any cost and will find many excuses to justify itself. It gets rid of reason with clever rhetoric bolstered by blame and demonizes others, for the ego has to *win* at all costs—because throughout millions of years of evolution, it *did* die if it did not get its wants and needs fulfilled. The ego has a long, long memory and millions of years of reinforcement.

∾

On its own, the ego would never seek salvation. . . . The mechanism for salvation is via the will, which invites the intervention of Divinity.

∾

With compassion, one realizes that the structure of the ego is such that it cannot know what lies beyond.

∾

Note that in a holographic universe, the achievements of every individual contribute to the advancement and well-being of the whole.

∾

The ego structure is dualistic and splits the unity of Reality into contrasting pairs and seeming opposites that are therefore the product and content of perception, which consists of projections.

∾

The only protection is owning that we are the source of our own experience, that we are the master of it, that we can handle it, and that we are greater than it.

∾

The ego is not the actual reality or source of life or existence, and is therefore vulnerable to dissolution. It is primordial but not essentially sovereign. It is dominant only until its illusory quality is recognized.

∾

Addiction to the ego's proclivities is like intoxication where pleasure is derived from the emotional payoff of negativity. Thus, negative positionalities tend to be self-perpetuating habits akin to addiction, based on presumptions and the inner seductive lure of the gratification of basic animal instincts. By repetition, they eventually gain dominance and control, which is the innate purpose of the narcissistic ego in the first place.

∽✧∾

The ego's position propagates itself because its secretly sought payoff is the emotion itself.

∽✧∾

The ego is oriented toward specifics and the linear content of the field of vision. Its effect on vision itself is exclusive and limited in order to focus primarily on the near side of objects (so as to facilitate manipulation). Spirit is oriented toward context and the whole, and is thus inclusive and focused on the far side of objects. Its field is diffuse rather than local.

∽✧∾

The ego is addicted to being "right" (for example, politics). A prevailing goal of the ego is to be "right." Therefore, it is the core of the payoff of righteousness. You can be right without being righteous, and you can be righteous without being right.

∽◡∽

The sense of "who" we are is primarily an identification with the body, the personality, and its mental processing, with accompanying emotional investment. One can do an internal mental imaging process to see how much of the body or its sensations could actually be lost and yet have the self retain a sense of "I." It becomes clear that the experiential "I" *has* a body but is *not* a body.

∽◡∽

The attachment to the body is to sensation and the superimposition of the concept of "mine"; what is "mine" and is controlled by "me" must therefore be "who I am." Identification with the body is consequent to the ego's positionalities. To detach from identification of the self as the body, it is necessary only to see the body as an "it" rather than a "me."

∽◡∽

The self identifies not only with the mind, but also with its content—which becomes "my" memory, "my" senses, "my" thoughts, "my" emotions, "my" property, "my" success, "my" failure, "my" expectations, "my" feelings, and so on. Identification presumes ownership and authorship; thus, the ego sees and believes itself to be a personal, separate causal agent and the inferred source of its own existence.

∞

All the great teachers have declared that man's primary defect is "ignorance." Research reveals rather quickly that the underlying basis of this ignorance is due to the limitation of the innate structure of the ego itself as a consequence of the still-ongoing evolution of consciousness.

∞

The vanity of the ego (at the level of pride) is endless and vainglorious in its grandiose delusion that it can disprove the existence of God. Cognition is only linguistic supposition confined to linear symbols, the limited content of mental processing. That it has any actual objective reality at all is a purely subjective presumption.

∞

The absolute subjectivity of revealed Truth precludes all considerations or uncertainties, which stem only from the ego. When the ego collapses, all argument ceases and is replaced by silence. Doubt *is* the ego.

∾

By spiritual endeavor, one discovers that it is *oneself* who has been a captive and a "victim" ensnared by the clever deceptions of the ego.

∾

Paradoxically, benefit is derived by the self-interest of the ego when it begins to realize that there is a great advantage to unselfishness. When it learns of the benefit of letting go of egocentric goals, the ego itself then becomes the springboard to spiritual inquiry and the means to its own transcendence, realizing that humility is strength and not weakness, and that it is wisdom and not ignorance. The willingness to "forgive and forget" calibrates at 450 (reason/logic). The willingness to "forgive and surrender to God" calibrates at 540 (unconditional love).

∾

Like the body, the mind is not one's real self, and like the body, it is basically impersonal. It has thoughts, but these thoughts are not a product of the self. Even if a person does not want a mind, he or she has one anyway. There is no choice in the matter; the mind is imposed and thrust upon one unasked. The fact that having a mind is an involuntary imposition helps with the realization that it is not a personal choice or decision.

∞✑∞

Through self-examination and inward focus, one can discover that all states of consciousness are the result of the execution of an option. They are not unchangeable certainties determined by uncontrollable factors at all. This can be discovered by examining how the mind works.

∞✑∞

Cease to identify with the body/emotions/mind as "me." Be truthful and admit that they are yours but not you. This may seem artificial, strange, foreign, and unnatural in the beginning; yet the basic reality is that it is a truth of higher order, which makes it a very powerful and formidable tool. The mind will try to deny this reality as well as truth (that's what it is "supposed to do") because Truth is intuited as its nemesis.

∞✑∞

As a term, "principles" may sound abstract, but the consequences of principle are quite concrete. If we examine principles, we will see that they reside in an invisible realm within consciousness itself. Although we can point out examples of honesty in the world, honesty itself as an organizing principle central to civilization is nowhere independently existent in the external world. True power, then, emanates from consciousness itself; what we see is a visible manifestation of the invisible. . . . Meaning is so important that when life loses meaning, suicide commonly ensues. When life loses meaning, we first go into depression; when life becomes less meaningful, then we finally leave it. Force has transient goals; when those goals are reached, there remains the emptiness of meaninglessness. Power, on the other hand, motivates us endlessly. If our lives are dedicated, for instance, to enhancing the welfare of others and everyone we contact, our lives can never lose meaning.

∽◌∽

One of the basic principles of consciousness itself is its intrinsic innocence. Because the mind is innocent, we have to begin to carefully watch and guard it. We have to become like its mother. The mind is like an innocent child who goes out in the world and believes everything it hears. It believes every billboard, every commercial, and every remark that people make. It believes what it sees. It has no way to evaluate it and has no sense of discrimination. We have to begin to take responsibility and say, "I can see that my mind is intrinsically innocent, and because the innocence of the mind of the child is still with me throughout life, I should start looking into what it has been buying."

∽✦∾

Unless there is an underlying attractor pattern, nothing can be experienced. Thus, the entire manifest universe is its own simultaneous expression and experience of itself.

∽✦∾

All seeming separation is an artifact of thought. It is essential to see that the mind is at all times experiencing a point of view.

∽✦∾

If you watch what your mind is really doing, you'll see that it is always trying to get "one up" on the next instant. By the next instant (about 1/10,000th of a second), what a person is experiencing (they are never experiencing reality) is the ego's interpretation of reality. Like an audio system, there is a monitor. So just as you record a program, the monitor feeds it into your ears. You hear what was just recorded a split second ago, but you are not hearing the program source; you are hearing what was just recorded.

Most people experience the monitor tape of the ego's interpretation of events. They're not experiencing events as they are in reality; they're experiencing the ego's interpretation.

∽✤∽

The primary defect now is, as it always has been, that the design of the human mind renders it intrinsically incapable of being able to tell truth from falsehood. This single, most crucial of all inherited defects lies at the root of all human distress and calamity.

∽✤∽

All negative emotions persist because of their secret payoff. When this "ego juice" is declined, thoughts tend to diminish and then disappear. The mind then tends to "go blank," which then brings up the fear of boredom. With observation, it becomes clear that the mind is busy anticipating the future (fear); clinging to the past (regret, hatred, guilt); or savoring the past to extract pleasure via reruns. Thus, the mind becomes the focus of amusement as "doing" something.

∾

In looking at this from the viewpoint of Truth, we can see there is no such thing as "just ego." It would mean that there is some place where God is not. All positions represent ego, and the ego is then superimposed on that which is not ego. There has to be something larger, which is consciousness itself. To safely do spiritual work and avoid crises, it is necessary to reaffirm, look within, and discover one's own innocence. It really is not safe to do spiritual work unless one has a glimpse of that innate naïve innocence and keeps one eye on it at all times, because that innocence is the gateway back to the Truth so one does not get lost in the swamp.

∾

The mind has only information and imagination *about* anything; it cannot actually "know" because to know is to be that which is known. All else is only speculation and supposition. When the mind is transcended, there is nothing left to ask about. That which is complete lacks nothing, and that completion is self-evident in its Allness.

PART II

SURRENDERING THE SELF

Love is a way of being. It is the energy that radiates when the blocks to it have been surrendered. It is more than an emotion or a thought—it is a state of being. Love is what we have become through the pathway of surrender.

෴

One is not really ruled by the mind at all. What the mind reveals is an endless stream of options, all disguised as memories, fantasies, fears, concepts, and so on. To get free of domination by the mind, it is only necessary to realize that its parade of subjects is merely an arbitrary cafeteria of selections wending their way across the screen of the mind.

෴

Letting go greatly facilitates the power of affirmations. An affirmation is a positive statement. Its power is limited by the fact that, either consciously or unconsciously, we have multiple negative programs that are saying the very opposite thing to the affirmation. You can discover this for yourself by noticing that, as you write the affirmations, your mind comes up with, "Yeah, but . . ." It is these "Yeah, buts . . ." that limit the power of the affirmation and reduce its effectiveness. If you surrender the obstacles to the affirmation, you will notice a rapid increase in their effectiveness.

∾

In actuality, the ego-self doesn't have to die at all: life doesn't come to an end; existence doesn't cease; and no horrible, tragic fate is waiting to end life at all. Like the ego itself, the whole story is imaginary. One doesn't have to destroy the ego or even work on it. *The only simple task to be accomplished is to let go of the identification with the ego as one's real self!*

With this relinquishment of identification, the self actually goes right on walking and talking, eating and laughing—the only difference is that, like the body, it becomes "that" instead of "me" or "this."

All that is necessary, then, is to let go of ownership, authorship, and the delusion that one invented or created this self and see that it was merely a mistake. That this is a very natural and inevitable mistake is obvious. Everyone makes it, and only a few discover the error and are willing or able to correct it.

∾

As Buddha said, "Put no head above your own," meaning that one's only true guru is the Self (the Buddha nature).

The Self of the teacher and one's own Self are one and the same. The teacher becomes a source of inspiration and information. It is the inspiration that supports the quest.

∽

The human mind is like a ship at sea that is unable to correct its direction without a compass or an external source of reference, such as the stars. It is important to realize that a system is only correctible when it has access to an external point of reference (like a global positioning system) that serves as the Absolute by which all other data are compared.

∽

Through observation, it can be seen that beneath the images and words themselves, there is a driving energy—a desire to think, to stay mentally active, to keep busy with any input the mind can find to fill in the gaps. One can detect a drive to "thinkingness," which is *impersonal*. With observation, one can detect that there is no "I" thinking the thoughts at all. In fact, the "I" rarely intervenes.

∽

The mind will get critical and try to save face by ridiculing a higher state. This is a golden opportunity because this is the very attitude that prevents a person from reaching that higher state of life. The very process of reading this material is invaluable, for it will reveal precisely what the blocks are and exactly why these goals are impossible at the present time. As resistances, criticisms, and disparagements come up, we can begin surrendering them and letting them go right now in the process of reading about them. It is a great opportunity to identify the inner blocks to fulfillment. As Pogo said, "We have identified the enemy, and it is us."

∽

Integrous morality and ethics, like genuine reason and faith, are firmly grounded in realistic humility by which essence supersedes appearance and socialized perception. Morality as a virtue is represented by the ethics of character traits, such as consideration for others, honesty, integrity, accountability, and responsibility, as well as allegiance to basic spiritual concepts. To be benign, affectionate, supportive, polite, kind, considerate, and helpful does not raise the flag of a cause or of being superior. Morality is thus a humble way of being in the world for its own sake rather than for gain or ego inflation. The consequences are internal but also evidenced by degrees of happiness and realistically based self-esteem.

∞◎∞

At all times, remain aware that the real you is not the ego. Refuse to identify with it.

∞◎∞

The first tools we need are willingness and an open mind—the willingness to say that the mind is looking at something which it is being asked to view so it can be healed. The healing of the body comes about with the healing of the mind. All the physical illnesses, which I eventually let go of, finally healed of their own nature as a result of healing the thought forms in mind. All the healings resulted from the willingness to let go of the condemnation of self and others, to let go of criticalness, self-pity, resentment, and all the negative energies at the levels below 200, including regret, worry, anxiety, grievances, self-contempt, and self-hatred. It was the letting go of those things that shifted the energy field to one that brought about the healing.

∞◎∞

The ego is not overcome by condemnation, hatred, and guilt. Rather, one de-energizes it by viewing it objectively for what it truly is—that is, a vestigial remnant of man's evolutionary origins.

∽

The key to success is to study and imitate a truthful authority rather than resist or attack it through competitive envy, jealousy, or hostility.

∽

Reality becomes self-evident when the obstruction of perception and mentation are removed, including all belief systems.

∽

It is not necessary to know about the Self but simply to become it by letting go of the non-Self. The realization comes about as a subjective transformation.

∽

Blind faith, the truth of a teaching, and the integrity of the teacher, plus dedication and adherence to a simple practice, are all that are required. . . . With the realization that the intellect is no longer a useful tool but now the barrier, the seeker arrives at the ripeness

which is necessary for the more focused paths to God
by transcending the mind, either via the heart or via
the pathway of consciousness.

∾

The key to transcending the inherent limitations
of the ego/mind is humility, without which the mind
is hopelessly trapped in its illusory house of mirrors.

∾

Like the sun, the inner Self is always shining,
but because of negative clouds, we do not experience it. It is not necessary to program oneself with
the truth; it is only necessary to remove that which
is false. The removal of the clouds from the sky to
illuminate the negative allows one to experience the
energy fields of that which is positive. It is only the
removal of the negative that is necessary—the willingness to let go of the habits of negative thinking.
The removal of the obstacles to the experiencing of
this will result in an increasing sense of aliveness
and a joy of one's own existence.

∾

The first illusion to surrender is the belief that
there is such a thing as "mind." Experientially, one

can only state that thoughts, feelings, images, and memories come into one's awareness in an endless progression. The word "mind" is therefore only a concept, as is the word "ego."

∿

Letting go of the ego is based on the willingness to surrender attachment to it as a substitute for God and just another illusion.

∿

How can meditation persist in one's daily existence? By merely constantly posing the question to oneself of "what" is doing the acting, talking, feeling, thinking, or observing. This is a focus of attention, with no languaging. . . . Continuous meditation could be likened to a mudra, or posture and attitude, in which every act is sanctified by its surrender as an act of service or worship. When one's attitude towards everything becomes a devotion, Divinity reveals itself.

∿

One sacrifices material or egocentric gain for spiritual progress, and in so doing, the transient is subordinated to the permanent, and that which is of true value is chosen over that which is only an illusion.

A yardstick that is helpful in making decisions is to project oneself ahead to one's deathbed and ask, Which decisions do I want to be accountable for at that time?

∾

The love of God by worship, devotion, commitment, declaration, or selfless service is the catalyst and the formal invitation for the intercession of Divinity via the power of the nonlinear field of consciousness itself, which is omniscient, omnipresent, and omnipotent. By surrender of all resistances, this powerful nonlinear field becomes progressively dominant and eventually an all-encompassing Presence.

∾

With the style of detached observation, the unfolding of life reveals itself to be the consequence of the spontaneous emergence of actuality as a manifestation of potentiality when conditions are favorable.

∾

All true religions reaffirm that salvation is a consequence of surrendering to and acknowledging God through faith, worship, good deeds, prayers, and declaration.

∽✦∾

If, in the exact passing moment of each instant, there is a complete willingness to totally surrender to it, one can suddenly transcend the ego in a flash. And then the way opens for Realization, wherein the Light of God as Self reveals the Source of all Existence and Reality.

∽✦∾

Consciousness advances itself when it is provided with essential information that then becomes activated by intention. This in turn prompts inspiration, humility, and surrender, and these tendencies become progressively more operative. When dominant, they lead to dedication and perseverance. In addition to these aspects of consciousness, progress is greatly aided by expert guidance and the usefulness of the calibrated levels of consciousness of the teachers and the teachings.

∽✦∾

Illusion is the secondary, automatic consequence of positionality. What happens in a miraculous transformation is that the positionality dissolves, allowing for a greater contextualization, outside of time and place, by which the linear content is replaced with the nonlinear (context).

∽

When carefully examined, one finds that all opinions are worthless. They are all vanities and have no importance or intrinsic merit. Everyone's mind is loaded with endless opinions, and when seen for what they are, opinions are really only mental activity. What is of more importance, however, is that opinions stem from and reinforce positionalities, and it is these positionalities that bring on endless suffering. To let go of positionalities is to silence opinions, and to silence opinions is to let go of positionalities.

∽

The evolution of consciousness is one's karmic inheritance because it is a quality innate to human consciousness itself. . . . The value of watchful witnessing is that even just awareness of an ego defect tends to undo it. By surrender and prayerful invocation, Divine Will facilitates transition from the lesser to the greater, for the Self effortlessly supports and energizes intention.

∽

The totality of the self is held within a larger underlying nonlinear field of awareness that is always present. It represents context rather than content. By analogy, it would be like looking at the planet Earth from outer space, where space is the context and Earth is the content. . . . With surrender, obstructions are dissolved by the infinite compassion of Divinity that unconditionally loves all that exists, for that existence is the manifestation of God. Only illusions could make this obvious truth not apparent.

❧

Error occurs when we cling to the belief that I *am* "that." Truth is unveiled when we see that one *has* "that" or *does* "that," instead of *is* "that."

❧

When it learns of the benefit of letting go of ego-centric goals, the ego itself then becomes the springboard to spiritual inquiry and the means to its own transcendence, realizing that humility is strength, not weakness, and that it is wisdom and not ignorance.

❧

The ego—or more accurately, the belief that one *is* the ego—obscures the Realization of the Reality of the Self as the Oneness of All That Is. The dissolution of the ego results in liberation from the bondage of the illusions that create suffering. These illusions are susceptible to fearless scrutiny that reveals the underlying fallacies. The only tool needed is the willingness to unreservedly surrender all beliefs, opinions, and attitudes to God.

∽◈∾

The activation of spiritual potentiality is a consequence of nonresistance, which is like the flower that opens and responds to the warmth of the sun by virtue of its intrinsic qualities imbued by Creation itself.

∽◈∾

It is not really necessary to subdue the ego but merely to stop identifying with it.

∽◈∾

The clever ego can extract the juice/payoff of secret gratification and pleasure from anything it arbitrarily selects. Actually, it is always just the same goal over and over again. The "what" that is desired is actually irrelevant. The locus is imagined to be "out there" but is actually "in here," for the pleasure gained is subjective and internal. The relinquishment of this single, solitary goal unveils the Reality of the Self—which is the innate prime source of all happiness—and its Realization terminates all wants and desires. The locus of happiness is always solely from within. Pleasure is transitory; joy and happiness are from within.

∽

To watch the mind from a detached position is educational and nonstressful, and it can be done with equanimity.

∽

From thinking that we *are* our minds, we begin to see that we *have* minds—and that it is the mind that has thoughts, beliefs, feelings, and opinions. Eventually we may arrive at the insight that all our thoughts are merely borrowed from the great database of consciousness and were never really our own. Prevailing thought systems are received, absorbed, and identified with; in due time, they are replaced by new ideas that have become fashionable with us. As we place less value on such passing notions, they lose their capacity to dominate us. We experience progressive freedom of, as well as from, the mind. This in turn ripens into a new source of pleasure; fittingly, the pleasure of existence itself matures as one ascends the Map of Consciousness.

∽✑∾

All thinking, from a spiritual viewpoint, is merely vanity, illusion, and pomposity. The less one thinks, the more delightful life becomes. Thinkingness eventually becomes replaced by knowingness. That one "is" does not really need any thought at all. It is helpful, therefore, to make a decision to stop mental conversation and useless babbling.

∽✑∾

Once thoughts, like objects, are depersonalized, they become devalued and lose their attraction. Thoughts and feelings arise from desire, and the mind desires what it values.

To clear the mind, merely note that nothing at all is of special or unique "value" or "worth" except by invested, superimposed, and projected belief. Therefore, withdraw value, worth, importance, and interest.

∽✑∾

With practice, one can stay focused on the quality of consciousness as a process without actually getting involved in the "what" that is being processed or experienced.

∼✦∽

Those who have tried Zen meditation know that the first thing taught is the handling of discomfort of the physical body by letting go of resisting the experience, cancelling out thoughts about it, and becoming one with it, thereby disappearing it.

∼✦∽

If the goal of life is to do the very best one can do at each unfolding moment of existence, then through spiritual work, one has already escaped the primary cause of suffering. In the stop-frame of the radical present, there is no life story to react to or edit. With this "one-pointedness" of mind, it soon becomes obvious that everything merely "is as it is," without comment or adjectives.

∼✦∽

The essential nature of spiritual work is to stay focused on what arises from instant to instant and become aware of "what" is experiencing and where it is being experienced.

∾⟊∾

The intent of meditation is detachment, especially detachment from the notion that thoughts are "mine" or represent "me." In Reality, they are merely "its," as is the mind itself. The idea of ownership arises from the personalization of these thoughts due to familiarity because the mind (like a camera) was present to record these past thoughts, events, and memories. However, it recorded them only because they were imbued with importance. Note that little roadside detail is recalled from a boring cross-country drive. The mind's inner camera records what is valued.

∾⟊∾

A useful decision or choice is to decide to stop mentally talking about everything and refrain from interjecting comments, opinions, preferences, and value statements. It is therefore a discipline to just watch without evaluating, investing worth in, editorializing, commenting, or having preferences about what is witnessed.

∾⟊∾

Every life experience, no matter how "tragic," contains a hidden lesson. When we discover and acknowledge the hidden gift that is there, a healing takes place.

~~~

As the payoffs of the ego are refused and surrendered, its grip on the psyche lessens, and spiritual experience progresses as the residues of doubt are progressively relinquished. As a consequence, belief is replaced by experiential knowledge, and the depth and intensity of devotion increase and may eventually supersede and eclipse all other worldly activities and interests.

~~~

Letting go of the old is facilitated by willingness, courage, and faith. Spiritual progress literally benefits all mankind in that it raises the general level of consciousness. Even one iota makes a difference. Another obstacle to spiritual growth is impatience. This can be overcome by surrender.

~~~

When the mind stops talking, one is aware that one *is* life. One is immersed in it rather than being on the surface, talking about it. Paradoxically, this enables full participation. With diminution of ego-centricity, the joy of freedom and the sheer flow of life sweep one into total surrender. One then stops reacting to life so that it can be enjoyed with serenity.

∾

One has the illusion that one couldn't get through life unless one thinks. No such thing happens. It is not necessary for any individual to be there. It is not necessary to think that there is an "I" that is responsible for one's actions. Everything is doing itself. It is the vanity of the ego that says, "I did this; I thought that; I decided that." There is no such "I" at all.

∾

By understanding and accepting the nature of the ego, it is transcended and finally collapses and disappears when all of its positionalities and their resultant dualities have been surrendered. The ego does not become enlightened but instead disappears and collapses. It is then replaced by a Transcendental Reality as described by the Buddha; that is, the Buddha Nature. Just as the sun shines forth when the clouds disappear, the Reality of the Self shines forth of its own as Revelation, Realization, and Enlightenment.

Simply put, realization or enlightenment is the condition where the sense of self moves from the limited linear material to the nonlinear infinite and formless. The "me" moves from the visible to the invisible. This occurs as a shift of awareness and identification from perception of form as objective and real to the realization of the purely subjective as the Ultimate Reality.

Curiosity can be shifted from the form and content of thoughts in order to become aware of the silent nascent field of consciousness/awareness itself. Silence is of the Self; thoughts are of the self.

In the process of spiritual discovery, one looks to discover what it is that is aware of—and has the authority to sense the existence of—"I-ness" or the quality of "I-ness," rather than a specific or circumscribed "me" as the "I."

Spiritual intention subserves, reinforces, and focuses on witnessing and observing rather than on "doingness" or specifics. Spiritual processing is like positioning oneself in the wind or in a water current.

∞∽

One-pointedness of mind means to focus on the crest of the wave of witnessing/experiencing, plus being willing to surrender perceived loss or gain. That is the primary skill that is needed.

∞∽

The purpose of meditation is to transcend the mind and its mental activities and limited perceptions, thereby transcending duality and becoming increasingly aware of Oneness.

∞∽

It is simple to observe that although there is a "talking mind" going on at the same time, there is also a silent awareness that is more global and unfocused and operates automatically. Contemplation or meditation that focuses attention on context rather than content facilitates moving one's identity from the transient and volitional (thereby becoming personal) to the unchanging quality of awareness itself.

This leads to the discovery that one is the field and not the specifics of the content. This jump in realization can be very sudden, which is a level of the Buddhist state of *satori*.

∽✧∾

The ego often seems to collapse in a piecemeal fashion. Once faith in the reality of the ego as being the true self is undermined, its dissolution has already begun. When one's loyalty and allegiance is shifted from the ego to the ultimate reality of God, a space is created. Into the opening flows God's Grace, as represented by the Holy Spirit.

∽✧∾

The spiritual student is often seeking to transform, overcome, or slay the ego, when all that is necessary is to simply abandon it. This requires the development of trust, faith, and confidence in the Reality of God. When the seeking for gain is abandoned, life becomes relatively effortless and peaceful.

∽✧∾

The ego equates survival of life with control. In a final surrender of control, the underlying primordial fear arises. Life is a consequence of the Divinity of its Source, which is the ultimate confrontation to the very core of the ego.

～✧～

To undo the grip of the mind requires a radical humility and an intense willingness to surrender its underlying motivations. This willingness receives energy and power from another willingness—the one that arises from the love of God—and the passion for surrendering love of thought for love of God.

～✧～

Everyone already at a certain level knows that they "are"—the ego then quibbles about the details of definition, but the Self is not fooled by the ruse. All false identifications can be dropped in an instant with the willingness to surrender all mental activities to God.

～✧～

In Reality, everything is spontaneously manifesting the inherent destiny of its essence; it doesn't need any external help to do this. With humility, one can relinquish the ego's self-appointed role as savior of the world and surrender it straight to God. The world that the ego pictures is a projection of its own illusions and arbitrary positionalities. No such world exists.

❧

Traditionally, the pathways to God have been through the heart (love, devotion, selfless service, surrender, worship, and adoration) or through the mind (*Advaita*, or the pathway of nonduality). Each way may seem more comfortable at one stage or another, or they alternate in emphasis. Nevertheless, it is a hindrance to consider that there is a personal self or an "I" or an ego that is doing the striving or seeking, or that will become enlightened. It is much easier to realize there is no such thing as the ego or an "I" identity that is doing any seeking; instead, it is an impersonal aspect of consciousness that is doing the exploring and seeking.

❧

The basic purpose of spiritual work and dedication is to transcend the innate evolutionary limitations of the ego and thereby access and develop the nascent capacity of consciousness itself, which bypasses all the limitations of the ego/self. Truth then presents itself by virtue of Divine Grace. Divinity reveals Itself to those who call upon It in God's time. The pace of spiritual evolution can seem slow, but spiritual endeavor is never futile. Progress can become very sudden and very major in dimension and impact.

∾

All the truth that is necessary to know has already been spoken by actual beings on this planet. All Great Teachers proclaim the same truth, for there is none other. The Radiance of the Self within beckons one on and provides spiritual inspiration and strength. The Presence of God within is the source of one's existence; therefore, to seek one's source is in accord with God's Will.

∾

The option for truth, peace, and joy is always available—although it's seemingly buried behind an ignorance and non-awareness that results from having chosen other options as a habit of thought. The inner truth reveals itself when all other options are refused by surrender to God.

THE
DIVINITY
OF THE
SELF

Spiritual commitment is energized by the alignment of the spiritual will (calibration level 850) with the attributes of Divinity, which are truth, love, compassion, wisdom, and nonpartiality. Devotion prioritizes one's life and attracts that which is of assistance. To be a servant of God is a dedication whereby the goal takes precedence over all other positionalities, attractions, or distractions.

∾

In the energy field of love, we are surrounded with love, and that brings gratitude. We are thankful for our life and for all the miracles of life. We are thankful for the doggies and the kitties, because they represent love. We are grateful for every act of kindness from others, their affection, caringness, and thoughtfulness.

∾

To understand the nature of God, it is necessary only to know the nature of love itself. To truly know love is to know and understand God, and to know God is to understand love.

∾

That which is ultimate and eternal transcends both objectivity and subjectivity and is beyond awareness. It is referred to in the ancient spiritual literature as "the Supreme Spirit." Out of the Supreme arises all that is manifest and unmanifest; all consciousness and awareness; all existence; All That Is; either form or nonform; all that is linear and all that is nonlinear; all that arises out of creation; all possibility and actuality. The Supreme is beyond existence or nonexistence; beyond beingness or is-ness; beyond all Gods, heavens, or spiritual forms; beyond all names or definitions; beyond all divinities and spiritual denotations. It is out of the Godhead that Divinity arises, and out of the Supreme arises the Godhead.

∽✦∽

It is not possible to arrive at truth and ignore consciousness because truth is the very product of consciousness.

∽✦∽

That which is Reality is beyond all form and yet intrinsic to it. Let form reveal its own nature—there is no need to seek it. The actual essence of form is formlessness, as paradoxical as that may sound.

∽✦∽

Every loving or compassionate thought outweighs many thousands of negative thoughts held by others. We change the world not by what we say or do but as a consequence of what we have become. Thus, every spiritual aspirant serves the world.

∽

The Self is the awareness—its source, its completion, its totality, its fulfillment, and its essence. It is the Reality of Reality, the Oneness and Allness of Identity. It is the ultimate "I-ness" of consciousness itself as the manifestation of the unmanifest. Thus, only can the indescribable be described.

∽

There is an invisible, all-encompassing energy field of love that surrounds everyone. Therein resides the higher Self or spirit through which the individuals, in varying degrees of consciousness, contact awareness or, unfortunately, may be cut off from it altogether.

∽

The straightest way to spiritual evolution and advanced states of consciousness is via the field of consciousness itself, which is the nonlinear Radiance of Divine Energy that is the substrate of all that exists. The condition of enlightenment is the state of pure Radiance that shines forth as the Presence/Self.

∾

Life is the radiance of God made manifest, as the universe expressed through evolution. We are both the product and the witness of Creation as a continuous, eternal process.

∾

All that is truly of God brings peace, harmony, and love and is devoid of all forms of negativity. Spiritually aware persons realize that they can only carry the message, for it is the inner truth that is the teacher.

∾

The ultimate source of existence has no cause nor does it have a beginning or an end. The closest appropriate description is conveyed by the terms "foreverness" or "alwaysness." This unique quality is forever present and available as a major subjective quality of the Reality of enlightenment.

∾

Beyond the level of 500, material possessions and worldly needs become irrelevant, which is why true teachers neither seek nor desire material gain.

∽✦∽

All things are in a state of silent rejoicing that their consciousness is an experience of Divinity. Unique to all things is a still, ever-present gratitude that they have been granted the gift of experiencing the presence of God. This gratitude is the form in which worship is expressed. All that is created and has existence shares in reflecting the glory of God.

∽✦∽

There is absolutely nothing in ordinary human experience to compare with the joy of the Presence of the Love of God. No sacrifice is too great, nor effort too much, in order to realize that Presence.

∽✦∽

Identification solely with the content of consciousness accounts for the experience of self as limited. In contrast, to identify with consciousness itself is to know that one's actual self is unlimited. When circumscribed self-identifications have been surmounted so that the sense of self is identified as consciousness itself, the condition is called "enlightened."

❧

Every thing and every event is a manifestation of the totality of All That Is, just as it is at any given moment. Once seen in its totality, everything is perfect at all times and nothing needs an external cause to change it in any way.

❧

What does the Self feel like? It is central, solid, profound, still, immutable, nonlocal, diffuse, all encompassing, peaceful, tranquil, comfortable, secure, emotionless joy, infinite lovingness, protection, closeness, safety, complete fulfillment, and ultra-familiar.

❧

The Self is Self-aware beyond the senses. Divinity shines forth as a massive revelation. Its obviousness is stark and forceful as a radiance. Its essence is certainty and finality, totality and completeness. All searches have ended.

❧

The Presence of God as Love is self-revealing as the duality of perception ceases as a consequence of surrendering positionalities. Love is therefore the doorway between the linear and the nonlinear domains. It is the grand avenue to the discovery of God.

∾

From the viewpoint of enlightenment, one might say that the linear is observed from the context of the nonlinear. To put it differently, existence is the manifestation of Divinity as form. In and of itself, the universe is therefore harmless. The viewpoint from enlightenment transcends the experiencer, the observer, the witness, and even awareness itself.

∾

There is no division between Creator and that which is created. All is self-creating as the manifestation of the mind of God. This great awareness characterizes the consciousness level of the 700s on the Map of Consciousness, where Self is All That Is. Because the universe is self-evolving and self-fulfilling, no intervention is necessary. All is in perfect balance and harmony.

∾

The Profound Peace prevails in the Silence, which marks the ending of the experience of time. The illusion of time precludes Peace in that it occasions an expectation of a feeling of loss or anticipation.

∾

All experience is thus simultaneously that of content (perception, images, thoughts, feelings, etc.) illuminated by the nonlinear field of context (the light of consciousness/awareness). . . . It is critical to differentiate the substrate infinite energy field of consciousness/awareness itself (cal. 600 and above) from its limited linear mental content (e.g., thoughts, images, feelings, and memories).

∾

God is All Present, simultaneously as manifest and unmanifest, as void and Allness, as visible and invisible, as the potential and the actual, as the expressed and the unexpressed.

∾

The mercy of God is infinite and unconditional.

∾

True happiness arises from the nonlinear. With relinquishment of dependence on the experiencer for pleasure and happiness, one discovers that the source of happiness is one's own existence, and the realization of the Self is happiness itself.

To cease identifying the experiencer as the reality of oneself is a major transition from dualistic content to nondualistic context, and therefore, from self to Self.

Because the ego deals in form and definition, it cannot comprehend the Self—which is beyond all form, but without form would not appear to exist. In Reality, there is neither subject nor object; therefore, there is no relationship to be explained.

The ultimate awareness and knowingness in the Presence of God is Peace. That Peace proclaims infinite safety and preservation with infinite protection. No suffering is even possible.

Truth is radical subjectivity. With the collapse of the illusions of duality—including the supposed "reality" of a separate "self"—there remains only the state of the Infinite "I," which is the manifestation of the Unmanifest as the Self.

∾

Complete surrender to God unveils the Truth. Nothing is hidden; only the ego is blind. Reality lies just beyond the mind. Out of the fear of becoming nothing, consciousness denies its only reality that it is everything—the infinite, everlasting Allness out of which existence itself arises.

∾

In contrast to the ego's perception of God, the Absolute Reality of the Self is the manifestation of God as the very core of one's existence. The love of the Presence is ultrapersonal and experienced as infinite peace, infinite security, and the safety of foreverness so that there is no imaginary "end" to fear. The God of the Presence imbues the joy of completion. Love is not a "quality" of God but is God's very essence.

∾

Just as the successful mountain climber relies on basic tools plus a map, a guide, and the experience of others, the seeker of Truth relies on the accumulated wisdom and verifiable reality, which is knowable by the actual process of Realization itself. It is this specific condition of Realization that is the true teacher and the Source of the teachings of the sage.

∽✦∽

The Realization of the Presence of Divinity unfolds of its own when the ego and its perceptual positionalities are surrendered.

∽✦∽

Whether one linguistically considers God to be called "Rama," "Brahma," or "Allah" is really irrelevant —God is not limited by any positionality or ascribable qualities. Likewise, God is not subject to the duality of either/or, which would have to be the basis of any favoritism.

∽✦∽

The realization that we are the source of our happiness, and that we can create it at any second, gives us a sense of completion. The sense of completion

THE EGO IS NOT THE REAL YOU

runs concomitantly with the experience of life, so it can be cut off at any second yet still feel complete.

∾

The true Self is invisible and has no characteristics by which it can be judged. It has no describable qualities, nor can it be the subject of any adjectives at all. The Self merely *is* and is beyond verbs, adverbs, and adjectives. It does not even "do" anything.

∾

Exceptional subjective experiences of truth, which are the province of the mystic, affect all mankind by sending forth spiritual energy into the collective consciousness.

∾

Realization is not a "gain" or an accomplishment, nor is it something that is "given" as a reward for being good—these are all notions from childhood. God is immutable and cannot be manipulated into granting favors, or seduced by bargaining or adulation. Worship benefits the worshipper by reinforcing commitment and inspiration. God is still, silent, and unmoving.

∾

To know that the Self is context and that, in contrast, the self is content is already a huge leap forward. The naïve seeker merely keeps reshuffling the content.

∽◌◊◌∾

The Self is beyond, yet innate in, all form—timeless, without beginning or end, changeless, permanent, and immortal. Out of it arises awareness, consciousness, and an infinite condition of "at home-ness." It is the ultimate subjectivity from which everyone's sense of "I" arises. The Infinite Reality does not even know itself as "I" but as the very substrate of the capacity for such a statement. It is invisible and all-present.

∽◌◊◌∾

The Self is not conditional; it has no qualities and is not dependent or explicable. The Self has no duration, beginnings or endings, location, form, or limitations. It is the Radiance of the Self that illuminates existence, without which there would be no awareness. The Self is beyond process. All descriptions are inappropriate and inapplicable to the Self.

∽◌◊◌∾

The spontaneity of life is an expression of essences interacting effortlessly. The miracle of Creation is continuous, and all life shares in the Divinity of its Source, for nothing comes into existence except by Divine ordinance. Once the sacredness of life is revealed, there follows the knowingness of what is meant by the phrase, "Gloria in Excelsis Deo!"

❧

Enlightenment is not a condition to be obtained; it is merely a certainty to be surrendered to, for the Self is already one's Reality. It is the Self that is attracting one to spiritual information.

❧

The source of the Self is the reality of Divinity. Although it is the source of existence, it is not subject to it, nor is such a term applicable.

❧

Life itself is not subject to cessation but only to change of form. The Source and essence of life is God, Who is not subject to demise. One cannot lose one's source. Death is the end of one chapter of a series of stories that finally cease only when the ego-author surrenders to its source.

∽◦∼

The Self is like one's inner grandmother who watches over a child so he does not forget to take his raincoat or mail the rent check. God is not ominous but loving; fear arises from the imagination.

∽◦∼

The Presence of the Self is complete, permanent, and totally fulfilling—it has no needs. Everything occurs spontaneously as an expression of its intrinsic essence. There is nothing and no one to "cause" anything to happen.

∽◦∼

In reality, the Love of God, like the sun, shines equally on all.

∽◦∼

The Presence as Self illuminates the Allness of Reality. Everything is equal by virtue of the Divinity of its existence as the Infinite Supreme, out of which all existence and creation arise. There is no selectivity or division; all is of equal value and importance.

∽◦∼

The Self knows, by virtue of its essence, all that exists beyond time and therefore beyond memory.

～◊～

The Presence of Self constitutes the classic *purusha*, or Radiance of Self as Source. Self "knows" by virtue of identity with Divinity itself. It thereby is its own Awareness, and by its Presence, it thereby makes itself "known" as the "Knower." Thus, it does not know "about," but is the completion of its own essence.

～◊～

The realization and knowingness of God is radically and purely subjective. There is not even the hypothetical possibility that reason could arrive at Truth. Truth is knowable only by virtue of the identity of being it.

～◊～

The Allness of Divinity is strongly confirmed by the immense power of Love as intrinsic to Creation and Divinity. The Presence of Love is all-pervasive and experienced as one's intrinsic Self. It melts linearity into Oneness, which is simultaneously exquisitely gentle and—paradoxically—infinitely powerful. Love is the Ultimate Law of the Universe.

∾

Through inner observation, there is the realization of something that remains constant and the same, no matter what goes on in the external world or with body, emotions, or mind. With this awareness comes a state of total freedom. The inner Self has been discovered. The silent state of Awareness that underlies all movement, activity, sound, feeling, and thought is discovered to be a timeless dimension of peace.

∾

Divinity is the Source of all Existence, including one's own.

∾

Truth is autonomously self-evident by virtue of its existence as Allness.

∾

Life, like existence, has no opposites—just as truth has no opposite, self-existent pseudo-reality such as falsehood. Truth is either present or not. Divinity, God, Allness, Oneness, and the Absolute are All That Is; no opposite to God can exist. Only the truth is true; nothing else exists. All fear, then, arises from attachment to form due to the illusion that form is a necessary requirement for existence.

∾∾

With awareness of Reality, all learning stops. The mind becomes silent. In peace and stillness, all that exists radiates forth its own meaning and truth and reveals that the nature of existence is stunningly divine. Everything radiates forth its Divine essence as Existence itself. That which Is and that which is Divine are one and the same.

∾∾

Truth is the radical simplicity and obviousness of God. It is unity. The word "unity" signifies the completeness of the Self-identity of existence. All is complete by virtue of being itself. No descriptions or nominal designations are required; they are all distractions. Even to just witness requires no thought. There is no necessity to mentalize Reality; it does not enhance what *is* but instead detracts from it.

∾∾

Truth is actuality; nontruth is false because it never existed and therefore was never recorded, which is why it exhibits a "false" (absence of truth) response to consciousness-research testing. Consciousness only responds to what "is" or "has been" in Reality. The source of consciousness is the Absolute Reality, classically called Truth.

❦

The only energy that has more power than the strength of the collective ego is that of Spiritual Truth.

❦

The power of Truth itself is a quality of Divine Love that, in its infinite mercy, dissolves positionalities back into the Reality of the Self.

❦

There is no separation between Creator and created, no subject or object; they are one and the same. Such terms as "new" or "old" are only nonexistent points of view, like "now" or "then." We are the constant witness to Creation at the very moment of Creation itself. What we witness is the Hand of God as experience. Awareness is the "Eye" or witness, and Creation is the handiwork of the infinite Self.

❦

In the Presence of God, all suffering ceases. One has returned to one's Source, which is not different from one's own Self. It is as though one had forgotten, or is now awakened from, a dream. All fears are revealed to be groundless; all worries are foolish imaginings. There is no future to fear, nor past to regret. There is no errant ego/self to admonish or correct. There is nothing that needs changing or improving. There is nothing about which to feel ashamed or guilty. There is no "other" from which one can be separated. No loss is possible. Nothing needs to be done, no effort is required, and one is free from the endless tug of desire and want.

∽

Begin by accepting the very important statement that *all truth is subjective.* Do not waste lifetimes looking for an objective truth, because no such thing exists. Even if it did, it could not be found except by the purely subjective experience of it. All knowledge and wisdom are subjective. Nothing can be said to exist unless it is subjectively experienced. Even a supposedly purely objective material world, if it existed, could be said to exist only because of one's subjective sensory experience of it. Even the most rabid materialist is stuck with the fact that in the end, it is only their own subjective awareness that gives it the authority of believability.

∽∾

Awareness merely registers what is being experienced; it has no effect on it. Awareness is the all-encompassing attractor field of unlimited power identical with life itself.

∽∾

Falsity is not the opposite of truth but merely its absence. In reality, truth has no opposite, just as cold is not the opposite of heat, nor is light the opposite of darkness.

∽∾

The Ultimate is the realm of nonform, nonlimitation, and nonlocality; therefore, it is the realm of the totality of the ever-present All.

∽∾

There is only Existence. Existence requires no cause, and to think as much is to create a fallacy of logic. By Existence, we mean discernible through observation, and it imputes a hypothetical change of condition from nonexistent to existent. However, that which is *always* was in its completeness beyond all time; looking for a "primary cause" is an artifact of mental activity that arises along with the concepts of time and space. Beyond time and space, there are no events, no beginnings, and no endings that are beyond the categories of human thought or reason.

∽◎∾

The first evidence of the Presence of God is an awakening curiosity or interest in spiritual matters. That is the crack in the ego's dam. When the person begins to desire or practice spiritual goals or pursue spiritual information, the Presence is already taking hold of his life.

∽◎∾

The discovery of the Presence of God is not due to fear but to the surrender that was precipitated by the fear.

∽◎∾

With the cessation of time, the doors swing open to an eternity of joy; the Love of God becomes the Reality of the Presence. The Knowingness of the Truth of all Life and Existence stands forth with stunning Self-revelation. The wonderment of God is so all-encompassing and enormous that it surpasses all possible imagination. To be at last truly and finally home is profound in the totality of its completeness.

∾

The Presence of God is the quintessence of profound peace, stillness, and love. It is overwhelming in its profundity. It is totally enveloping, and the love is so powerful that it dissolves any remaining "non-love" held by the residual ego.

∾

The infinite presence of all things is beyond all time and space, forever complete, perfect, and whole. All points of observation disappear, and there is the omnipresence of that which Knows All by the fact that it Is All. As Reality stands forth in its stunning self-evidence and infinite peace, it appears that the block to Realization was the mind itself, which is not different from the ego—they are one and the same.

∾

The term "Self" emphasizes that God is discovered within as the Ultimate Reality that underlies one's actual existence in the "here and now" (to quote the Bible: "The Kingdom of God is within you").

⟿

To surrender identification with that which was presumed to be "me" allows the Real Me to shine forth as the immanent quality of Divinity that is the source of the unencumbered reality of "I."

⟿

The sense of "I" is an identification and a know-ingness that are qualities of the Inner Presence, which enable the capacity to know the "I" as Self. Stripped of all pretenses, the inner sense of "I-ness" merely knows Itself without any content.

⟿

No concepts are possible in the Infinite Light of the glory of God. There is a profound peace, safety, and "at home-ness." Completion has finalized.

⟿

The prevalence of inner silence is the threshold of the dawning realization that everything is happening of itself and that nothing is causing anything; one becomes aware that such constructions are merely forms of mental entertainment.

❧

One can realize the Self as the primordial, irreducible Reality from any starting point. It is not the starting point that is important but the dedication to relentlessly pursuing it to its very roots. To unravel the nature of experience leads to one's Source. Any leg of the elephant leads to the elephant.

❧

The infinite field of the Source of All Existence is a radiant effulgence that shines forth, and its consequences as Creation are forever unified. Creator and Creation are one.

❧

The experience of Divinity within as Self, or God Immanent, is quite different from belief in God Transcendent. It is for this reason that the Buddha counseled against all depictions or nominalizations of God, because enlightenment is a condition or state in which the Self-knowing is that of Identity. In this condition or state, there is no "this," such as self, with which to describe the Self. The condition or state is best described as "Self-effulgent," and in that state the Knowingness is its own Reality.

∾

The ego/mind is a learned set of behaviors, and the ultimate goal is to transcend its programming and functioning by virtue of the power of the Radiance of the Self, which recontextualizes life benignly. The Presence of the Self is experienced as compassion for all of life in all its expressions, including its evolution as one's personal self. As a consequence, forgiveness replaces condemnation, which is a sign that it is now safe to proceed deeper into serious inner inventory without undue stress.

∾

To be at one with phenomena, instead of separate from them, results in experiencing the aliveness and Allness of the Presence expressed as All That Exists. All that has existence is not just passively "there" but instead seemingly presents itself to awareness as a quality of its existence rather than as a volitional intention. Thus, the universe appears to be a gift of exquisite beauty and perfection that shines forth with the intrinsic Radiance of Divinity.

∾

Divine Love is an all-inclusive field, and its quality is unforgettable, as anyone who has ever had a near-death experience knows. It is intrinsically truly ineffable, and its Presence is like a meltingness in its exquisite, experiential totality. There is nothing in worldly life that even comes close to it. It is profoundly gentle, yet infinitely powerful by virtue of its intrinsic infinite strength.

❧

Innate to the Presence as Love is the quality of timelessness/foreverness. Even a brief moment of the Presence in earthly time is realized via the Self to be eternal. This is an unmistakable hallmark. Therefore, to have known the Real for even a few brief moments of clock time is to know it forever.

❧

Divinity is Infinite Love. Within its Presence, even relinquishment of bodily existence is not a "problem" or a source of resistance. . . . As the ego dissolves, so do all its fears and presumptions. The Inner Reality is immune to considerations or doubts. The Self is Certainty.

❧

The Radiance of God is the light of awareness that reveals the Divinity of all that exists. In the stillness of the Infinite Presence, the mind is silent, as there is nothing that can be said; all speaks of itself with completeness and exactitude. With this realization, one transcends the final duality of existence versus nonexistence because only existence is possible. The opposite of Truth does not exist, since Reality excludes nonreality. In this realization resides the Peace of God.

∾

Fear itself actually precludes the awareness of the Presence of God. Only when it is abandoned does profound surrender of the resistant ego reveal a peace beyond understanding.

∾

There is nothing more wonderful than arriving back home again at one's Source. The illusion is that one struggles with spiritual growth by one's own effort; in fact, we are pulled into greater awareness by the Will of God expressed as the Holy Spirit, and all that is necessary is to allow it to happen by surrendering completely. For truly, only God is God.

∾

Eventually even the illusion of witness/observer dissolves into awareness/consciousness itself, which is discovered to be nonpersonal and autonomous. There is no longer the limitation of "cause and effect" or "change." The illusion of "time" also dissolves into the Allness of Divine Concordance. There is neither attraction nor aversion to existence itself, for even the manifest is seen to be a consequence of discernment by consciousness as a concept.

∽

An analysis of the nature of consciousness reveals that redemption occurs as the result of the return of consciousness to its original pristine state of nonduality. It can do so only by the "obedience" of surrendering the dualities of will and willfulness of the ego to the nonduality of God's Truth. The return from the duality of the ego to the nonduality of the spirit is so difficult and unlikely that only by Divine Grace is it even possible. Thus, man needs a savior to be his advocate, his inspiration, and the fulcrum of his salvation from the pain and suffering of the ego.

∽

Ego/mind *thinks*, field (consciousness) *knows*, and Self *is*.

∾

Nonduality means without form, division, or limitation—such as time, locality, or mentalization—including arbitrary linear presumptions. Divinity is, by its innate "qualities," omniscience, omnipresence, and omnipotence; and all evolves as a consequence of the Unmanifest's becoming Manifest as evolutionary Creation.

∾

In Reality, from a nondualistic viewpoint, it can be observed and experienced that everything is actually occurring spontaneously as the field effect of the automatic consequence of the manifesting of potentiality into actuality. Unseen is the underlying power of the infinite context of Consciousness/Reality/Divinity and its effect on content. The nonlinear, infinite field of power is equally present within, without, and beyond. Potentiality becomes actuality when conditions permit or are favorable. The process is empowered by intention, as well as by the innate impersonal quality of consciousness itself.

∾

In the nonduality of awareness, even sequence no longer occurs, and awareness replaces experiencing. There is no longer the experience of "moments," as there is only a continuous Now. Movement appears as slow motion, as though suspended outside of time. Nothing is imperfect. Nothing actually moves or changes; no events actually take place. Instead of sequence, there is the observation that everything is in a stage of unfoldment, and that all form is only a transitional epiphenomenon created by perception and the observational habits of mental activity.

In Reality, all comes into being as an expression of the infinite potentiality of the universe. Evolving states are the consequences of conditions but are not caused by them. Conditions account for appearances, and the phenomenon as change is really the result of an arbitrary point of observation.

∽

In the Reality of nonduality, there is neither privilege nor gain nor loss nor rank. Just like a cork in the sea, each spirit rises or falls in the sea of consciousness to its own level by virtue of its own choices—not by any external force or favor. Some are attracted by the light and some seek the darkness, but it all occurs of its own nature by virtue of Divine freedom and equality.

∿

Inasmuch as the entire universe and everything in it is a karmic unity, the Allness of Reality is the realization of enlightenment. If all is a karmic unity that originates from the same source, then to see any separation is an artifact of perception. In Reality, the one and the many are the same.

∿

The small self is dissolved by the Self. The healing attitude of the Self to the self is compassion; it is through forgiveness that one is forgiven. This willingness to surrender, arising out of the Grace of God, permits the power of God expressed as the Holy Spirit to recontextualize understanding—and, by this device, to undo the reign of perception and its attendant duality, which is the source of all suffering. The dissolution of duality is the ultimate gift of God, for it dissolves the very source and capacity for suffering. In nonduality, suffering is not possible.

∿

On the level of nonduality, there is observing but no observer, as subject and object are one. You-and-I becomes the One Self experiencing all as Divine.

❧

Within nonduality, positionality is not possible; thus, dualistic perceptions stemming from positionalities are the source of the misunderstandings about God for which, unfortunately, mankind has paid a great price.

❧

To transcend the linear to the nonlinear is the way of the mystic—the pathway of nonduality—to realize the inner light of consciousness itself, the True Immortal Self. Everyone trusts the inner sense of reality or capacity to "know" that underlies all experiencing and witnessing, no matter what the content. The content of mind thinks, but only the nonlinear field "knows," or how else would it be possible to know what is being thought?

Because everyone actually lives in the experiential at every moment, the Source of the capacity to know or experience is close at hand and is itself pristine. All human beings experience that they are continuously "experiencing," no matter what the ever-changing content might be.

❧

All humans are already mystics and innately attracted to enlightenment, whether they are aware of it or not. It is an extension of the qualities of learning and curiosity, which are innate to the mind. Thus, the pathway of "Devotional Nonduality" is open to everyone and has no requirements, other than the capacity for inner honesty and the willingness to align with verifiable truth and follow it to its Source.

∽

The knowingness that arises from within is innate, accessible, and experiential. Such knowingness is also beyond definition or description as the primary, confirmable, universal substrate of power and energy—out of which arises the possibility as well as actualization of existence. This Ultimate Reality is revealed via the search into the substrate and source of consciousness itself, which is the ultimate nonlinear context beyond all definition. Thus, via the pathway of enlightenment, there is no separate relationship of "you-God" vis-à-vis "me-human."

∽

In Devotional Nonduality, the likelihood of error is bypassed by devotion to the essential nonlinear qualities of Divinity itself, such as compassion, oneness, love, truth, omniscience, eternal, infinite, omnipresence, and omnipotence—beyond form, place, time, human instincts, or emotions.

While the primary prerequisite for adherence to religion is faith, the essential required qualities needed for following the pathway of nonduality are humility, surrender, and devotional dedication to the pathway.

It is readily observable that followers of religions are characterized by the presumption of "I know" via scriptural authority, ecclesiastical doctrine, historical precedent, and so on. In contrast, the spiritual devotee for nonduality starts from the basic, more truthful position that "I, of myself, *don't know*."

To adopt the pathway of Devotional Nonduality recontextualizes the obligation to the pursuit of Truth rather than worldly involvement and action. How best to serve the world is concordant with comprehension.

Commitment is to the core of Truth itself, and it is free of seduction by proselytization or secrecies. All that is necessary is a curiosity and attraction to Truth—which is complete, total, and self-sufficient.

∾

Even the simplest action, such as peeling a potato, can be accompanied by resentment or by devotion to life out of joy, knowing that one is supporting life through life. In gratitude for the gift of life, one dedicates that life back as a gift to God through selfless service to His creation as all of life. With this dedication, one validates the sacredness of all life and treats it with respect.

∾

The universe responds to love by revealing its prevalence. It is hidden to ordinary perception, but the awareness is finessed by lovingness itself. Awareness is a capacity that is beyond the senses or emotions. If one ceases anthropomorphic projections and limitations, it is revealed that all that exists is innately conscious and emanates love as a consequence of the divinity of Creation.

∾

It is important to know that consciousness has no particular space, no physical area, and no limitation. The common fantasy is "I experience things in my head." Actually, we do not experience them in the head. Where do we experience a thought? We experience a thought nowhere; there is no specific location or space in which we experience a thought. The nature of consciousness is that it has no particular form; it is without form. Its content is with form, but the field of consciousness itself is like space, having no particular locality.

∾

Ultimate Truth is realized as pure, radical subjectivity. It is self-revealing and beyond argument.

∾

The great teachers taught the Truth about Divinity, not religion, which came centuries later. While the veneration of religion and scriptures is understandable, it is their truth and God that are meant to be worshipped and sought.

∾

A religion primarily addresses the realm of duality, whereas enlightenment addresses nonduality. This strict path to enlightenment says that inasmuch as duality is illusion, there is no point in trying to perfect it. Therefore, the ego is to be transcended and seen for the illusion that it is. "Good personhood" is laudable, but it does not of itself result in enlightenment. The possibility of reaching enlightenment is based on advanced understanding of the nature of consciousness itself.

❦

To even hear of enlightenment is already the rarest of gifts. Anyone who has ever heard of enlightenment will never be satisfied with anything else.

❦

Humor is an expression of freedom and joyfulness, and laughter is biologically healing. . . . Faith, love, and joy are the high road; doom and gloom merely lead to sadness and despondency. Self-hatred blinds awareness of the Self as a reflection of Divine Creation.

❦

That which I am is Allness. To realize that one already is and always has been All That Is leaves nothing to be added.

∾

The "Infinite I" is that subjective reality that underlies the individual "I" and allows for the experience of "I-ness" as one's existence. It is the absolute "I" that enables the statement, "I." Consciousness, or the capacity for awareness, is formless and is the backdrop from which form can be identified.

∾

The source of the highest Spiritual Truth is nonmental. The intellect has difficulty comprehending this critical fact because the mind is intrinsically dualistic and limited, expecting a "this" to come from a "that." In the advanced spiritual Reality, duality dissolves because the "this" *is* the "that." The seeker and the Sought become One with the transcendence of the limitation of duality; that is, Realization of the Self, Illumination, and Enlightenment.

∾

When the conditions—including mindset, intention, and dedication—are favorable, a decision may arise to drop everything in the world. One might then throw oneself totally into an all-out, "go for it," continuous, laser-like, focused surrendering of the perceiver/ experiencer aspect of the ego. This process takes one quite rapidly beyond the mind to the very "processing edge" of the experiencer.

This "processor" edge is the actual locus of the ordinary sense of "I-ness," and it creates a 1/10,000th-of-a-second delay between reality (the world as it is; Descartes's *res extensa*) and the world as it is perceived or experienced (Descartes's *res cogitans*). This separation is the crux and locus of the self's illusion of duality, which obscures comprehension of the intrinsic Reality of Nonduality (Self). With transcendence of the illusion of a separate, individual, personal self, there emerges the Radiance and Oneness of the Self— by which all life, whether denoted as subjective or objective, is recontextualized into Oneness.

∽♾∽

Enlightenment is merely the emergence of Truth when the obstructions to the realization of that Truth have been removed. By analogy, the shining of the sun is not conditional upon the removal of the clouds; it merely becomes apparent.

∽♾∽

The way to sudden enlightenment is through strict adherence to spiritual awareness and specifics of consciousness so that the personality (ego) is transcended rather than perfected.

∽◌∾

The term "enlightenment" is semantically correct. It is the recognition and realization that one's reality is the light of the Self—and that it stems from within as an awareness and profound, self-evident Reality.

∽◌∾

In Reality, time is merely an illusion and an appearance. No "time" is really wasted once one has chosen the spiritual goal. Actually, it makes no difference in the end whether enlightenment takes a thousand lifetimes or one. In the end, it is all the same.

∽◌∾

A "good person" is one thing; enlightenment is another. One is responsible for the effort and not the result, which is up to God and the universe.

∽◌∾

The essence of man includes the potentiality for enlightenment. Readiness implies that one has evolved through the lower levels of consciousness, so spiritual inspiration now becomes the spark that ignites the quest.

∽∾

To understand the nature of consciousness makes enlightenment possible. This essentially entails the realization of the difference between duality and nonduality, as well as how to transcend the realm of duality.

∽∾

The straightest way to enlightenment is by transcending the limitation of the ego/mind by dedication to verified Truth itself. This process is suitable for modern humankind and devoid of conflict with science and religion.

∽∾

When one stops identifying with either the body or the mind, the functions continue autonomously, but merely without an identification as "myself." The sense of authorship disappears. Ongoing survival is autonomous, and continuance is an expression of consciousness in its alliance with the Holy Spirit.

∽◌∾

From the viewpoint of consciousness and enlightenment, the reign of fear does not cease until the desire for existence itself is surrendered to God. In the silence that ensues comes a great realization that one's existence has always been due to the Presence of the Self, which has attracted from the Universe whatever is necessary for survival.

∽◌∾

Salvation requires purification of the ego; enlightenment requires its total dissolution. The goal of enlightenment is more demanding and radical.

∽◌∾

The seeking of enlightenment is a very major commitment—and is, in fact, the most difficult of all human pursuits. Enlightenment as the primary goal of one's life occurs in only one in ten million people.

∽◌∾

Clarify that it is not a personal "you" who is seeking enlightenment but an impersonal quality of consciousness that is the motivator.

∽◈∽

There is no separation in the Allness of Creation, so it is impossible for the created to be separate from the Creator. Enlightenment is therefore the revelation of the Self when the illusion of the reality of a separate self is removed.

∽◈∽

The road to enlightenment is not for bleating sheep. To be offended signifies that one is defended, which, in itself, signifies the clinging to untruth. Truth needs no defense and therefore is not defensive; Truth has nothing to prove and is not vulnerable to being questioned for an answer.

∽◈∽

The oneness of Self-identity is the substrate of the phenomenon known as Revelation or Realization. Enlightenment is the finalized state that ensues—and it is unconditional, total, and complete.

∽◈∽

The personal "I" is "content," whereas the "I" of Reality is context. By analogy, the cloud is subject to change and dissolution. Weather comes and goes, but the sky itself remains unchanged. Enlightenment is merely the shift of identity from the cloud to the sky.

∿

Enlightened awareness is best described as a state or a condition, a realm or a dimension. It is self-revealing and all prevailing. It eclipses and displaces mentation, which becomes unnecessary and would, in fact, be an interference and intrusion. Revelation is subtle, powerful, soft, gentle, exquisite, and all embracing. The senses are bypassed, and all perception of "this" or "that" disappears. It is also apparent that the entire content of revelation has been there all along and simply not experienced or observed. The vision of what "Is" in its totality is entirely "Known" by virtue of the Self already being All That Is. Identity confers absolute authority of knowledge. The observer, that which is observed, and the process of observation are all identical.

∿

To be enlightened merely means that consciousness has realized its most inner, innate quality as nonlinear subjectivity and its capacity for awareness.

∽◈∽

Be resolute on the level of absolutely no reservation. Avoid the lure of the astral realms. Beware of the wolves in sheep's clothing, for they are attracted to the devotee who is making significant progress. Do not accept anyone into your life who does not pass the calibratable level of Truth. Keep your spiritual goal ever in awareness, no matter what the activity. Dedicate all endeavors to God. Remember the true nature of God and avoid any teachings that state otherwise.

∽◈∽

The desire to search for God or enlightenment is already evidence of having been spiritually inspired. As the ego vacates, the Radiance of the Self uplifts and inspires. Henceforth, it is not possible to be alone. At the critical moment, spiritual commitment and dedication bring forth the unseen help of the Great Beings who are no longer in physical bodies—yet their energy stands at the great doorway of the final moment when one is sustained by the Holy Spirit and the wisdom of the teachers of Truth.

∽◎∾

The straightest way to enlightenment is through devoted introspection, meditation, and contemplation of the inner workings of the ego so as to understand consciousness. The process is energized by intention, dedication, and devotion; and the total effort is supported by spiritual inspiration. The dedication is focused on the process itself as a surrender to God. The focus needs to be intense, and it is energized by fixity and deliberateness of intention. The process is one of discovery and becomes progressively self-revealing.

∽◎∾

To follow the strict pathway to enlightenment is a specific discipline and commitment. It is not the same as practicing a religion. While there are many tenets of religion that support the search for enlightenment, there are also many that do not and actually constitute a hindrance. To be pious is one thing; to be enlightened is quite another.

∽◎∾

rtrt

tt

rtrtrt

tt

ttt

f f f

Here:

It is important to realize that the destiny of those who choose enlightenment is enlightenment—who else would be on such a quest? To merely seek spiritual purification and awareness is already a gift.

∽

Enlightenment means that the former personal identity and all that had been believed about it have been erased, removed, transcended, dissolved, and displaced. The particular has been replaced by the universal, qualities have been replaced by the nonlinear, and the discrete has been replaced by the unlimited.

∽

When enlightenment occurs, the ensuing state also completely reconstructs the appearance of the world. Everything is seen to happen of its own. There is no longer a "me" or a personal "I." The orientation to the world is completely altered, and functioning may be impossible or very difficult.

∽

In the state of enlightenment, all is self-revealing of its essence as its existence. Everything already is what it "means."

∽

Because no languaging of the state of enlighten-ment is actually possible, a Zen master may just sud-denly shout "Ha!" and hit you with a stick. What is hoped for is a sudden flash, during which the inexpli-cable Reality stands revealed.

∽✿∽

Enlightenment is the ultimate aesthetic aware-ness, for it allows the beauty of creation to shine forth with stunning clarity.

∽✿∽

Another simple analogy is that a shadow does not become a sunbeam, but is replaced by it. The ego is the shade; enlightenment is the consequence of the light of the Self that replaces it.

∽✿∽

Enlightenment is merely the full, conscious rec-ognition that innate Truth is the core of one's own existence—and that God as Self is the illumina-tion whereby that realization is made possible. The Infinite Power of God is the manifestation of the power of Infinite Context. The Unmanifest is even beyond Infinite Context.

∽✿∽

As the Buddha pointed out, being mortal automatically entails suffering, which is why he taught to seek enlightenment in order to preclude that karmically determined recurrence. At very high levels, the subjective experiencing of existence is no longer limited by the narcissistic ego or the psychological blocks of the positionalities. This condition is the consequence of progressive surrendering at great depths of all limitations and belief systems. The requirement is the persistent "one-pointedness of mind," processing out the emotional/mental residuals of lower consciousness levels and surrendering all self-identities and mental belief systems.

∿

The capacity to reach the condition or state classically called "enlightenment" represents the fulfillment of the potential of consciousness in its evolutionary progression.

∿

Consistent application of any spiritual principle can unexpectedly result in a very major and sudden leap to unanticipated levels. At that point, memory may not even be available; instead, the Knowingness of Spiritual Truth presents itself silently.

∽✸∾

Comfort and confidence can be derived from this verifiable reality: that the rare persons who are actually attracted to enlightenment as a life goal are attracted because that is already their destiny. For the same reason, only future golfers would be taking golf lessons.

∽✸∾

Enlightenment is the consequence of the surrender of all dualistic illusions to Truth. All suffering ends with dissolution of the ego's positionalities. Thus do we praise the Lord God for radiating Light to the world.

∽✸∾

To seek enlightenment is a major decision. The decision itself is therefore akin to a "yang" position— but subsequently, the process itself is more intrinsically akin to a "yin" posture. While the ordinary ego is programmed to "getting" (yang), spiritual intention now shifts to "allowing" (yin).

∽✸∾

The dedication to Self-realization and enlightenment is a disciplined straight-and-narrow path. Thus, a serious devotee is advised to bypass the attraction of curiosity and the appeal to the inner child offered by the magical and mysterious paranormal and psychic phenomena that are commonly merchandized and proffered as learnable skills.

∾

Spiritual evolution is a lifetime commitment and a way of life by which the world and all experience subserves spiritual intention. . . . Miraculous events are merely the actualization of potentiality that appears when conditions are appropriate. . . . From an even more advanced level of consciousness, it becomes apparent that all phenomena are actually occurring spontaneously as a consequence of the evolution of the universe itself, and therefore not only is life perfect at any moment, but it is also a continuous revelation in which one is a participant/observer.

∾

Aware mind is not prone to banal positionalities or judgments nor does it get entrapped in frenetic endeavors. It tends to be easygoing and mellow and prefers to observe rather than to become involved in the world's dramas. Aware mind is not involved in worldly definitions of gain or loss.

∽✿∾

The state of enlightenment is therefore the potential Reality that replaces the illusions of the ego's perceptual positionalities. Spiritual intention, effort, and decision potentiate the evolution of consciousness from the linear limited to the nonlinear Allness of Reality.

∽✿∾

God is the source and presence of peace, love, stillness, and beauty. God is beyond all universes and materiality, yet is the source of All That Is.

∽✿∾

To seriously seek enlightenment is a very strict discipline that therefore eschews the attraction of involvement in supposed spiritual movements that are actually intrinsically political in nature and factional. The attraction of "changing the world" (for the presumed better, of course) appeals to the naïve idealism of the inner spiritual adolescent and is transcended with maturity. The nature of human life is the automatic consequence of the overall level of human consciousness itself. Therefore, to benefit the world, it is necessary to change not the world but oneself—for what one becomes is influential by virtue of its essence (nonlinear) and not its actions (limited and linear).

∽

The energy of life is a radiance from the field of consciousness, which is the mode of the Presence of Divinity that manifests in physicality as Creation. The capacity for enlightenment is merely a consequence of consciousness returning to its source, which is Divinity Immanent as Self.

The ego/self identifies with its various functions and qualities and labels them as "me" and says that is "who I am." This results in the vanity of authority, an error that originated during evolution as a consequence of identification with the experience of the senses. Thus comes about a typical conclusion that "I" itch, instead of "the body" itches. The same error of authorship/ownership occurs with feelings and thoughts in that the witness identifies with the subject and the content of the experiencer.

The experiencer function is an information probe that collects linear data and therefore is an "it" and not a "me." It is a functional processing unit similar to the senses of smell or touch.

∽

Enlightenment is the consequence of a major shift of content and identification. The experiencer focus is like a screen that veils Reality and drops of its own accord when the props are removed. This is the consequence of surrendering the will to God. The sense of reality of the self was actually due solely to the underlying Presence of the Self.

∽◟◞

It is helpful to remember that neither Truth nor enlightenment is something to be found, sought, acquired, gained, or possessed. That which is the Infinite Presence is always present, and its realization occurs of itself when the obstacles to that realization are removed. It is therefore not necessary to study the truth but only to let go of that which is fallacious. Moving away the clouds does not cause the sun to shine but merely reveals that which was hidden all along.

Spiritual work, therefore, is primarily a letting go of that which is presumably known for that which is unknown—with the encouragement that the effort is more than well rewarded from others who have realized the Infinite Presence.

∽◟◞

To look within for the actual source of love leads to the discovery of the Self. Like the sun, the Self is ever present, unconditional, and not subject to thought, opinion, or attitude. The Self can only love because that is its essence. The love of the Self is not earned, deserved, or subject to limitation. The Self is the source of life and the subjective awareness of existence. . . . It is beyond all dualities; there is no duality between the Self and existence. The Unmanifest and Manifest are one and the same. Consciousness may include content, or it may not. By analogy, space is not dependent on the presence of planets or universes, yet it includes all of them.

∿

Consciousness does not recognize separation, which is a limitation of perception. The enlightened state is a "Oneness" in which there is no division into parts. Such division is only apparent from a localized perception; it is only an accident of a point of view.

∿

To best serve the world, seek enlightenment and transcend illusions rather than contribute to them.

∿

The Infinite, Ultimate Potentiality is the Actuality of Existence. "All That Is" is therefore innately Divine, or it could not exist at all. The absolute expression of Divinity is Subjectivity. If I exist, then God Is. Enlightenment is the verification that all existence is not only the result of Creation, but that existence itself is not different from the Creator. The created and the Creator are one and the same.

∽♨∾

Through spiritual alignment, intention, and devotion—aided by meditation, contemplation, authenticated instruction, and Truth; and assisted by the energy field of an advanced teacher—great leaps of consciousness can occur unexpectedly. Thus, it is important to know of these leaps well in advance, as confirmed by consciousness research.

The chances of becoming enlightened are now more than one thousand times greater than at any time in the past, which means that reaching the level of Unconditional Love (calibration 540) is a very attainable and practical goal. From the level of Unconditional Love, the pathway is increasingly joyful. At level 600, there occurs an infinite, silent stillness and peace—and progression from there is up to the Will of God, karma, and the potentialized Knowingness nascent within the spiritual aura.

∽∽

Truth is recognized. It presents itself to a field of awareness that has been prepared in order to allow the presentation to reveal itself. Truth and enlightenment are not acquired or achieved. They are states or conditions that present themselves when the conditions are appropriate and the obstacles are removed.

∽∽

All avenues of questioning lead to the same ultimate answer. The discovery that nothing is hidden and Truth stands everywhere revealed is the key to enlightenment about the simplest practical affairs and the destiny of mankind. In the process of examining our everyday lives, we can find that all our fears have been based on falsehood. The displacement of the false by the true is the essence of the healing of all things visible and invisible. And always, a final question will eventually arise for every questioner—the biggest question of all: "Who am I?"

∽∽

Investigation into the nature of consciousness leads directly to the very source of illumination, for the Light of Consciousness is the condition of enlightenment.

By its Light, the knower and the known are united in the realization of the Self as God Immanent.

∾

You have to let go of the illusion that you know who you are. In the Divine state, there is nothing to "know" about because you are it. That is a difficult leap to make—but suddenly, it occurs of its own accord, and then one is free forever. Uncertainty is replaced by endless delight. Human life is then an endless comedy! You're not a "who" but a "what."

∾

One reason for the seemingly endless delays on the way to enlightenment is doubt, which should be surrendered as a resistance. It is important to know that it is actually extremely rare for a human to be committed to Spiritual Truth to the degree of seriously seeking enlightenment, and those who do make the commitment do so because they are actually *destined* for enlightenment.

Who am I? Who is asking? You find out who is asking, and that answers the whole question. It's not a "who" but a "what."

∾

To not acknowledge the Presence of God would be to negate the Allness and Divinity of God; this is not possible for an enlightened being.

∾

At the last doorway to enlightenment stands the ego's final challenge, which is the central core belief that it is the source and locus of not only identity but also of life itself. At that point, one is all alone and shorn of all protection or comforting props, belief systems, or even memory. There is solely available within one's aura the high-frequency vibration of the consciousness of the Enlightened Teacher, with its encoded Knowingness. The last step is intuited as a finality from which no turning back is possible, and thus there is consternation at the absoluteness of the finality.

Then arises the knowing to walk straight ahead, no matter what, for all fear is illusion. As this last step is taken by the Spiritual Will, death is experienced, but the fierce anguish lasts for only a few moments. The death of the ego is the only actual death that one can possibly experience, in contrast to which the previous deaths of leaving the body were relatively trivial. The experience of death is terminated by awe at the revelation of the Ultimate Reality—and then even the awe disappears and the Self transcends the duality of Existence versus Nonexistence, Allness versus Nothingness, and Omnipresence versus Void.

∽✦∾

The serious student needs to know well in advance that at the very last doorway (Final Doorway calibrates at 999), he will be confronted by his willingness to surrender life itself—or at least that which has been believed since the beginning of evolution to be the very core of life itself. This final gateway is very rarely passed, and one reason is the lack of preparation, the lack of certainty, and a final doubt of major magnitude.

∽✦∾

In the end, to the true devotee, the pursuit of spiritual reality supersedes all other considerations. The commitment to become enlightened involves the decision *No matter what.*

∽✦∾

At the final moment, the last vestiges of doubt and existential fear may surface from the depths. At that point, faith in the teachings of the masters that direct us to "Walk straight ahead, no matter what" arises and proves to be correct, for the glory of God awaits on the other side of the last great barrier.

GLOSSARY

This glossary is a composite of edited excerpts from Dr. Hawkins's work.

Consciousness: Consciousness is the unlimited, omnipresent, universal energy field, carrier wave, and reservoir of all information available in the universe—and, more importantly, it is the very essence and substrate of the capacity to know or experience, to perceive or witness. Even more critically, consciousness is the irreducible, primary quality of all existence—the formless, invisible field of energy of infinite dimension and potentiality, independent of time, space, or location, yet all-inclusive and all-present.

Consciousness is an impersonal quality of Divinity expressed as awareness and is nondualistic and nonlinear. It is like infinite space that is capable of awareness and is a quality of the Divine Essence.

Context: The total field of observation predicated by a point of view. Context includes any significant facts that qualify the meaning of a statement or event.

Data is meaningless unless its context is defined. To "take out of context" is to distort the significance of a statement by failing to identify contributory accessory conditions that would qualify the inference of meaning.

Duality: The world of form characterized by seeming separation of objects, reflected in conceptual dichotomies such as "this/that," "here/there," "then/now," or "yours/mine." This perception of limitation is produced by the senses because of the restriction implicit in a fixed point of view.

Ego (or self with a small *s*): The ego is the imaginary doer behind thought and action. Its presence is firmly believed to be necessary and essential for survival. The reason is that the ego's primary quality is perception, and as such, it is limited by the paradigm of supposed causality. The ego could be called the central processing and planning center; the integrative, executive, strategic, and tactical focus that orchestrates, copes, sorts, stores, and retrieves. It can be thought of as a set of entrenched habits of thought that are the result of entrainment by invisible energy fields that dominate human consciousness. They become reinforced by repetition and by the consensus of society.

Further reinforcement comes from language itself. To think in language is a form of self-programming. The use of the pronoun "I" as the subject, and therefore the implied cause of all actions, is the most serious error and automatically creates a duality of subject and object.

Put another way, the ego is a set of programs in which reason operates through a complex, multilayered series of algorithms wherein thought follows certain decision trees that are variously weighted by past experience, indoctrination, and social forces; it is therefore not a self-created condition. The instinctual drive is attached to the programs, thereby causing physiological processes to come into play.

Enlightenment: A state of unusual awareness that replaces ordinary consciousness. The self is replaced by the Self. The condition is beyond time or space, is silent, and presents itself as a revelation. The condition follows dissolution of the ego. Everything is realized to be autonomous rather than the result of causality.

Karma: In essence, individual karma is an information package (analogous to a computer chip) that exists within the nonphysical domain of consciousness. It contains the code of stored information that is intrinsic to, and a portion of, the spiritual body or soul.

The core represents a condensation of all past experiences, together with associated nuances of thought and feeling. The spirit body retains freedom of choice, but the range of choices has already been patterned.

Karma is linear, propagates via the soul, and is inherited as the consequence of significant acts of the will. "Karma" really means accountability—and, as cited in previous spiritual research, every entity is answerable to the universe. To summarize, as is commonly known, karma (spiritual fate) is the consequence of decisions of the will and determines spiritual destiny after physical death (the celestial levels, hell, purgatory, or the so-called inner astral planes). Included also is the option of reincarnation in the human physical domain, which, as shown by consciousness-calibration research, can only be done by agreement with the individual will. So all humans have, by agreement, chosen this pathway. In addition, consciousness research confirms that all persons are born under the most optimal conditions for spiritual evolution, no matter what the appearance seems to be. You don't get born without your approval.

Linear: Following a logical progression in the manner of Newtonian physics and, therefore, solvable by traditional mathematics through the use of differential equations.

Nonduality: When the limitation of a fixed locus of perception is transcended, there is no longer an illusion of separation nor of space and time as we know them. On the level of nonduality, there is observing but no observer, as subject and object are one. You-and-I becomes the One Self experiencing all as Divine. In nonduality, consciousness experiences itself as both manifest and unmanifest, yet there is no experiencer. In this reality, the only thing that has a beginning and an ending is the act of perception itself.

Positionality: The positionalities are structures that set the entire thinking mechanism in motion and activate its content. Positionalities are programs, not the real Self. The world holds an endless array of positions that are arbitrary presumptions and totally erroneous. Primordial positionalities are: (1) *Ideas have significance and importance;* (2) *There is a dividing line between opposites;* (3) *There is a value of authorship—thoughts are valuable because they are "mine";* (4) *Thinking is necessary for control, and survival depends on control.* All positionalities are voluntary.

Self (capital *S*): The Self is beyond, yet innate in, all form—timeless, without beginning or end, changeless, permanent, and immortal. Out of it arises awareness, consciousness, and an infinite condition of "at home-ness." It is the ultimate subjectivity from which everyone's sense of "I" arises. The Infinite Reality does not even know itself as "I" but as the very substrate of the capacity for such a statement. It is invisible and all-present. The Self is the Reality of reality, the Oneness and Allness of Identity. It is the ultimate "I-ness" of consciousness itself as the manifestation of the unmanifest. Thus, only, can the indescribable be described.

Subjectivity: Life is lived solely on the level of experience and none other. All experience is subjective and nonlinear; therefore, even the linear, perceptual, sequential delineation of "reality" cannot be experienced except subjectively. All "truth" is a subjective conclusion. All life in its essence is nonlinear, nonmeasurable, nondefinable. It is purely subjective.

Truth: Truth is relative and only "true" in a given context. All truth is only so within a certain level of consciousness. For instance, to forgive is commendable, but at a later stage, one sees there is actually nothing to forgive. There is no "other" to be forgiven. Everyone's ego is equally unreal, including one's own.

Perception is not reality. Truth arises out of subjectivity and is obvious and self-revealing. Truth is radical subjectivity. With the collapse of the illusions of duality, including the supposed "reality" of a separate "self," there remains only the state of the Infinite "I," which is the manifestation of the Unmanifest as the Self. Truth has no opposites, such as falsity or "off-ness."

Nothing is hidden from the field of consciousness. The ultimate truth is beyond is-ness, beingness, or any intransitive verb. Any attempt at Self-definition, such as "I Am That I Am"—or even just "I Am"—is redundant. The Ultimate Reality is beyond all names. "I" signifies the radical subjectivity of the state of Realization. It is in itself the complete statement of Reality.

BIBLIOGRAPHY

Discovery of the Presence of God: Devotional Nonduality

Dissolving the Ego, Realizing the Self: Contemplations from the Teachings of David R. Hawkins, M.D., Ph.D.

The Eye of the I: From Which Nothing Is Hidden

Healing and Recovery

I: Reality and Subjectivity

Letting Go: The Pathway of Surrender

Power vs. Force: The Hidden Determinants of Human Behavior

Reality, Spirituality and Modern Man

Transcending the Levels of Consciousness: The Stairway to Enlightenment

Truth vs. Falsehood: How to Tell the Difference

ABOUT THE AUTHOR

David R. Hawkins, M.D., Ph.D. (1927–2012), was director of the Institute for Spiritual Research, Inc., and founder of the Path of Devotional Nonduality. He was renowned as a pioneering researcher in the field of consciousness as well as an author, lecturer, clinician, physician, and scientist. He served as an advisor to Catholic, Protestant, and Buddhist monasteries; appeared on major network television and radio programs; and lectured widely at such places as Westminster Abbey, the Oxford Forum, the University of Notre Dame, and Harvard University. His life was devoted to the upliftment of humankind until his death in 2012. Visit veritaspub.com.

Hay House Titles of Related Interest

We hope you enjoyed this Hay House book. If you'd like to receive our online catalog featuring additional information on Hay House books and products, or if you'd like to find out more about the Hay Foundation, please contact:

Hay House, Inc., P.O. Box 5100, Carlsbad, CA 92018-5100
(760) 431-7695 or (800) 654-5126
(760) 431-6948 (fax) or (800) 650-5115 (fax)
www.hayhouse.com® • www.hayfoundation.org

———

Published in Australia by: Hay House Australia Pty. Ltd.,
18/36 Ralph St., Alexandria NSW 2015
Phone: 612-9669-4299 • *Fax:* 612-9669-4144
www.hayhouse.com.au

Published in the United Kingdom by: Hay House UK, Ltd.,
The Sixth Floor, Watson House, 54 Baker Street, London W1U 7BU
Phone: +44 (0)20 3927 7290 • *Fax:* +44 (0)20 3927 7291
www.hayhouse.co.uk

Published in India by: Hay House Publishers India,
Muskaan Complex, Plot No. 3, B-2, Vasant Kunj, New Delhi 110 070
Phone: 91-11-4176-1620 • *Fax:* 91-11-4176-1630
www.hayhouse.co.in

———

Access New Knowledge.
Anytime. Anywhere.

Learn and evolve at your own pace
with the world's leading experts.

www.hayhouseU.com

Praise for *The Red Deal*

"The Red Nation has given us *The Red Deal*, an I[...]
practice that leads to profound changes in existi[...]
years of European colonialism, which produce[...]
relations, has nearly destroyed life itself. Techno[...] ...ed to reverse
this death march, but it will require a vision for the future and a path to follow
to arrive there, and that is what *The Red Deal* provides." —Roxanne Dunbar-Ortiz,
author of *An Indigenous Peoples' History of the United States*

"*The Red Deal* is an incendiary and necessary compilation. With momentum for
a Green New Deal mounting, the humble and powerful organizers of The Red
Nation remind us that a Green New Deal must also be Red—socialist, committed
to class struggle, internationalist in orientation, and opposed to the settler-
colonial theft of Indigenous lands and resources. Redistribution also requires
reparations and land back. *The Red Deal* is a profound call to action for us all."
—Harsha Walia, author of *Undoing Border Imperialism* and *Border and Rule:
Global Migration, Capitalism, and the Rise of Racist Nationalism*

"We really need *The Red Deal* because it forces open a critical conversation on
how land back can be a platform for mass mobilization and collective struggle.
The Red Deal poignantly argues that if we do not foreground decolonization and
Indigenous liberation in climate justice strategies such as the Green New Deal,
we will reproduce the violence of the original New Deal that dammed life-giving
rivers and further dispossessed Indigenous peoples of their lands. Strategically,
The Red Deal shows how, if we understand green infrastructure and economic re-
structuring as anticolonial struggle, as well as an anticapitalist one, we can move
from reforms that deny Indigenous jurisdiction towards just coalitions for repos-
session that radically rethink environmental policy and land protection without
sacrificing Indigenous life and relations." —Shiri Pasternak, author of *Grounded
Authority: The Algonquins of Barriere Lake Against the State*

"The world system, born in settler colonialism and racial capitalism, is mired in a
crisis at once ecological, epidemiological, political, and economic. What is to be
done? As this urgent book states, the choice is decolonization or extinction. *The
Red Deal* presents a rousing vision of a shared future of socio-ecological care, rooted in revolutionary Indigenous praxis. A must read." —Thea Riofrancos, author
of *Resource Radicals: From Petro-Nationalism to Post-Extractivism in Ecuador* and
co-author of *A Planet to Win: Why We Need a Green New Deal*

"*The Red Deal* offers a revolutionary program for global environmental justice informed by the liberation struggles and epistemologies of Indigenous, Black, migrant, and working people everywhere. The vision of this manifesto calls for nothing less than a radical transformation of our relationships with each other and the land itself. It is truly inspiring work that we have come to expect from our comrades in The Red Nation." —Glen Coulthard, author of *Red Skin, White Masks: Rejecting the Colonial Politics of Recognition*

"*The Red Deal* asserts that the fight for climate justice must center Native people when it comes to the issues that disproportionately impact Native communities, but it also communicates what the Green New Deal does not—namely, that public lands are stolen lands and climate change is significantly caused by just a few industries, which the government has at worst neglected to hold accountable and at best assisted in their efforts to mine the earth for resources in a move that put profits over people." —*Teen Vogue*

"The Red Nation also names Black abolitionists as an inspiration for the Red Deal, citing the links between mass incarceration and detention and climate change. They further note that police departments, prisons, and the U.S. military receive billions of taxpayer dollars annually while doing irreparable harm to Native Americans, Black people, and the Earth." —*Essence*

"The GND has the potential to connect every social justice struggle—free housing, free health care, free education, green jobs—to climate change. Likewise, *The Red Deal* places anti-capitalism *and* decolonization as central to each social justice struggle as well as climate change. The necessity of such a program is grounded in both the history and future of this land, and it entails the radical transformation of all social relations between humans and the earth." —*Jacobin*

"The Democratic Socialists of America is proud to endorse *The Red Deal*, an Indigenous centered set of policy recommendations that was written by The Red Nation. . . .The Red Nation is a group of radical Indigenous people that are fighting back against the US imperialist settler colonialist state. They are not just fighting for land and sovereignty, but for survival." —Democratic Socialists of America

"For the Red Nation, living and being interdependent with Mother Nature is explicitly anticapitalist. An ethos merely hinted at in the Green New Deal, *The Red Deal* understands that capitalism fundamentally protects wealth, not life" —*The Politic*

THE RED DEAL

INDIGENOUS ACTION TO SAVE OUR EARTH

THE RED DEAL

INDIGENOUS ACTION TO SAVE OUR EARTH

THE RED NATION

Brooklyn, NY
Philadelphia, PA
commonnotions.org

The Red Deal: Indigenous Action to Save Our Earth
The Red Nation

ISBN: 9781942173434
LCCN: 2021932193

10 9 8 7 6 5 4

Common Notions
c/o Interference Archive
314 7th St.
Brooklyn, NY 11215

Common Notions
c/o Making Worlds Bookstore
210 S. 45th St.
Philadelphia, PA 19104

commonnotions.org
info@commonnotions.org

Discounted bulk quantities of our books are available for organizing, educational, or fundraising purposes. Please contact Common Notions for more information.

The Red Nation
editor@redmedia.press
therednation.org

Cover design by Josh MacPhee / Antumbra Design
Layout design and typesetting by Morgan Buck / Antumbra Design
Antumbra Design www.antumbradesign.org

Contents

INTRODUCTION   1

Resistance   5

"New Deals"   8

Decolonization   12

Anti-Imperialism   13

The Red Deal   18

A Caretaking Economy   23

Demilitarization   25

Land Back   27

It's Not Just an "Indian Problem"   30

The Four Principles   31

   1. *What Creates Crisis Cannot Solve It*   32

   2. *Change from Below and to the Left*   34

   3. *Politicians Can't Do What Only Mass Movements Do*   36

   4. *From Theory to Action*   38

PART I

DIVEST: END THE OCCUPATION   43

Introduction   44

Area 1: Defund Police, Immigration and Customs Enforcement,
  Customs and Border Protection, and Child Protective Services   46

Area 2: End Bordertown Violence   51

Area 3: Abolish Incarceration (Prisons, Juvenile
  Detention Facilities, Jails, Border Security)   58

Area 4: End Occupation Everywhere   61

Area 5: Abolish Imperial Borders   66

PART II

HEAL OUR BODIES: REINVEST IN OUR COMMON HUMANITY   **73**

Introduction   74

Area 1: Citizenship and Equal Rights   77

Area 2: Free and Sustainable Housing   80

Area 3: Free and Accessible Education   83

Area 4: Free and Adequate Healthcare   85

Area 5: Free, Reliable, and Accessible Public
Transportation and Infrastructure   88

Area 6: Noncarceral Mental Health Support and No More Suicides!   91

Area 7: Healthy, Sustainable, and Abundant Food   93

Area 8: Clean Water, Land, and Air   95

Area 9: End Gender, Sexual, and Domestic Violence   98

Area 10: End Missing and Murdered Indigenous
Women, Girls, and Two-Spirit Peoples   102

PART III

HEAL OUR PLANET: REINVEST IN OUR COMMON FUTURE   **107**

Introduction   108

Area 1: Clean Sustainable Energy   112

Area 2: Traditional and Sustainable Agriculture   116
Land Return   121
Remediation   122

Area 3: Land, Water, Air, and Animal Restoration   124
Recommendations   126

Area 4: Protection and Restoration of Sacred Sites   128
Recommendations   130

Area 5: Enforcement of Treaty Rights and Other Agreements   131
Recommendations   134

Conclusion   135

CONCLUSION
OUR WORDS ARE POWERFUL, OUR KNOWLEDGE IS INEVITABLE   139
Infrastructures of Relation   139
The Power of Words   143

APPENDIX   148
Who We Are   148
Areas of Struggle   148
Principles of Unity   149

NOTES   152

ABOUT RED MEDIA   160

INTRODUCTION

There is something about the weather. Last year, bushfires in Australia scorched forty-six million acres—an area larger than Hungary and Portugal combined. Flames shot nearly a half mile in the air, killing thirty-four humans and more than one billion animals.

In the United States, over eight million acres burned, killing thirty-seven people and displacing countless others. Swarms of locusts darkened the sky in parts of East Africa and West Asia, devouring plants and fruits as they tore through the land, leaving hardly a scrap of green. A single living swarm in Kenya amassed to a size three times larger than New York City. Tens of millions of people across the globe faced increased food insecurity.

The weather was also surging in 2019. There were fever-pitched days of revolt in parts of Latin America and the Caribbean. Indigenous people came down from the mountains and forests, blockading capital cities. What felt like a strong breeze in Peru, Chile, Ecuador, Argentina, Honduras, Haiti, and Bolivia was forecasted by some to escalate into a "Bolivarian hurricane," a swirling storm of backlash against the failures of neoliberalism. In the evenings, the winds were brutally brisk. The nights were filled with terror and the howls of the families of the youth slain by sniper bullets, blinded by projectiles,

and beaten with police truncheons. The winds seemed to be blowing towards bloody reactionary violence.

In autumn 2019, a military coup backed by the United States deposed Bolivia's first Indigenous president, Evo Morales. His vice president, Álvaro García Linera, described the mood of his country as a forecast for the hemisphere:

> Like a thick night fog, hatred rages through the neighborhoods of Bolivia's traditional urban middle classes. Their eyes are brimming with anger. They don't shout, they spit. They don't make appeals, they impose their will. Their chants are neither hopeful nor fraternal, but they ring with discrimination and contempt for Indians (Indigenous Bolivians). They mount their motorcycles and saddle up in their SUVs, band together with their buddies from the fraternities and private universities, and set off hunting for the rebellious Indians who dared snatch power from their hands.[1]

Our Quechua comrade and relative Maya Ajchura Chipana told us that fear had gripped her people—Indigenous Bolivians—as *Wiphalas*, the symbol and flag of *Pachamama* [the Indigenous Andean Mother Earth], were burned in public. "It's like if they burned something sacred, like a little piece of your heart," Maya's father Juan Lazaro told her. "We refuse to be burned," Maya told us.

We know the stakes of our struggle. The horsemen of the apocalypse can't ride without a plague. The COVID-19 pandemic has swept across the globe, sharpening two competing visions of humanity—one based on science and caretaking, and the other on pure make-believe. The most powerful nation in the world chose the latter. Across the United States, Black, Brown, Indigenous, migrant, and poor people have borne the brunt of the virus. Even tepid social

reforms like universal healthcare—largely a reality for most nations of the Global North—was off the table. Instead, hundreds of thousands of people needlessly died, oftentimes alone, without access to the life-saving medications or treatments available to the super-rich. A large part of humanity perished, taking little pieces of our hearts with them. Others, who either survived the virus' symptoms or lost their jobs or homes—or all three—were left to fend for themselves as billionaires raked in record earnings.

In places like the Navajo Nation, rates of infection were exacerbated by centuries of resource colonialism, which has hobbled the Navajo economy, making it utterly dependent upon a dying industry that leaves nothing but poison and broken communities in its wake. While its rivers have been diverted to water golf courses in Phoenix and its mesas mined for coal to power the Southwestern US, about 30 percent of its population lives without running water and 10 percent live without electricity. Grandmothers who have been hauling water for ninety years live next to fracking rigs that pump millions of gallons of fresh water into the ground to crack it open for access to oil and gas, destroying the water and the land in the process. This is in a desert landscape where water is especially sacred and scarce.

In Indian Country, tribes that took the science of COVID-19 transmission seriously closed their borders and set up emergency health protections, all while being treated by white elites in reservation "bordertowns," towns that have sprung up outside reservation boundaries with notorious racist police forces and predatory relationships with Indigenous peoples and communities. Yet, the make-believe approach won over mostly white settlers and their leaders. Once it was revealed that the virus disproportionately impacted nonwhite communities, heavily armed men (most of whom

were white) stormed state capitols demanding haircuts and the reopening of restaurants. Others trespassed onto Native lands for vacations and outdoor adventures. As the virus intensified and spread, so did a toxic atmosphere of cynicism and hatred.

The coronavirus pandemic is like climate change, in the sense that the most advanced capitalist countries had ample advance warning about both threats—in addition to having access to the best scientific experts and holding a monopoly on resources—and did nothing. In May 2019, the US Department of Energy (DOE) announced it was officially renaming fossil fuels emitted into the atmosphere "molecules of US freedom." Similarly, the coronavirus' massive body count has been blamed not on the US' inhumane for-profit healthcare system, but on China as the virus' presumed country of origin. Because of its socialized healthcare system, China was able to swiftly manage the threat of the virus within a matter of months as it continued to spread elsewhere. Despite the massive tolls of death and destruction on its population, a viable strategy within mainstream North American politics has not coalesced. 2020 has been one of the hottest years on record, but as Maya said, with our hearts in our hand, we refuse to be burned. A different kind of storm has been gathering.

When the military forced Evo Morales from office in November 2019, he gave a speech: "We will come back," he said, quoting the eighteenth-century Indigenous resistance leader Tupac Katari, "and we will be millions." Not only had the coup government, with the support of the United States, overthrown Morales' administration, they also tried to crush the project for decolonization that it represented. When Morales returned, the social movements that had given rise to his administration blockaded the roads surrounding the major cities, effectively shutting down the economy. Millions forced the coup government to concede, and the Movimiento al

Socialismo—Instrumento Político por la Soberanía de los Pueblos (MAS) [Movement Toward Socialism] was overwhelmingly re-elected into power during the October 2020 general election. On November 9, Evo returned. With him, and the election of Luis Arce as president and David Choquehuanca as vice president, the Indigenous revolution continues.

This book takes as its primary inspiration the 2010 People's Agreement drafted in Cochabamba, Bolivia, a large part of the *proceso de cambio* [process of change] that MAS initiated. The agreement spells out principles of ecofeminism, ecosocialism, and anti-imperialism infused with traditional Indigenous ecological knowledge. This is the spirit of this book, *The Red Deal*, a manifesto and movement borne of Indigenous resistance and decolonial struggle. The weather is changing and so are the stakes; everyone feels the temperature rising.

Resistance

The pandemic all but erased how the Wet'suwet'en Nation stood up to Canada and Coastal GasLink Pipeline in early January 2020, kicking off a year of intense resistance. In February, the RCMP (Royal Canadian Mounted Police) removed Wet'suwet'en and Gitxsan matriarchs from the Unist'ot'en Camp by force. Police raided a healing center reconnecting Indigenous people to the land to help reverse the psychological and spiritual effects of ongoing genocide. Armed men forced their way through rows of red dresses set up by land defenders to honor the Indigenous women and girls who have gone missing or have been murdered on Canada's infamous Highway 16—known as the "Highway of Tears"—in so-called British Columbia. The cops ignored the dresses, just like

they have ignored the ongoing genocide against women and girls. What mattered to them was their historic duty: to clear Indigenous people from their land and make way for business. The Unist'ot'en Camp—whose motto was "Heal the People, Heal the Land"—stood in the way of the extractive economic giant that is Canada, a nation with a very public process to reconcile with First Nations, Inuit, and Métis peoples. The Wet'suwet'en matriarchs boldly declared that "Reconciliation is Dead" and called for a shutdown of the Canadian economy. Reconciliation is meaningless in a system where profits hold more sanctity than Indigenous life.

Indigenous peoples blockaded key railways across the country under the banner "Reconciliation is Dead." Nearly half a billion dollars' worth of goods sat idle for several weeks in February, disrupting supply chains for weeks, slowly bleeding the Canadian economy. It was the only language the settler state understood: money. Direct action focused on strategic chokepoints and co-ordinated with a mass mobilization of solidarity rallies, which forced the Canadian government to negotiate with Indigenous land defenders on terms it normally wouldn't consider. But more importantly, the Indigenous land defenders' demands became more focused. It wasn't just about "reconciliation" or stopping a pipeline. "People get confused about what we want as Native people," Denzel Sutherland-Wilson of the Gitxsan Nation said, referring to the eviction of the Coastal GasLink pipeline company from the lands of the Wet'suwet'en Nation. "It's like, 'What do you want?'. . . Just Land Back."[2]

The crux of the so-called "Indian problem" in the Western Hemisphere hinges on this question: "What do Indians want?" For us, it's a larger social problem of underdevelopment. Colonialism has deprived Indigenous people, and all people who are affected by it, of

the means to develop according to our needs, principles, and values. It begins with the land. We have been made "Indians" only because we have the most precious commodity to the settler states: land. Vigilante, cop, and soldier often stand between us, our connections to the land, and justice. "Land back" strikes fear in the heart of the settler. But as we show here, it's the soundest environmental policy for a planet teetering on the brink of total ecological collapse. The path forward is simple: it's decolonization or extinction. And that starts with land back.

In 2019, the mainstream environmental movement—largely dominated by middle- and upper-class liberals of the Global North—adopted as its symbolic leader a teenage Swedish girl who crossed the Atlantic in a boat to the Americas. But we have our own heroes. Water protectors at Standing Rock ushered in a new era of militant land defense. They are the bellwethers of our generation. The Year of the Water Protector, 2016, was also the hottest year on record and sparked a different kind of climate justice movement. Alexandria Ocasio-Cortez, herself a water protector, began her successful bid for Congress while in the prayer camps at Standing Rock. With Senator Ed Markey, she proposed a Green New Deal in 2019. Standing Rock, however, was part of a constellation of Indigenous-led uprisings across North America and the US-occupied Pacific: Dooda Desert Rock (2006), Unist'ot'en Camp (2010), Keystone XL (2011), Idle No More (2012), Trans Mountain (2013), Enbridge Line 3 (2014), Protect Mauna Kea (2014), Save Oak Flat (2015), Nihígaal Bee Iiná (2015), Bayou Bridge (2017), O'odham Anti-Border Collective (2019), Kumeyaay Defense Against the Wall (2020), and 1492 Land Back Lane (2020), among many more.

Each movement rises *against* colonial and corporate extractive projects. But what's often downplayed is the revolutionary potency

of what Indigenous resistance stands *for*: caretaking and creating just relations between human and other-than-human worlds on a planet thoroughly devastated by capitalism. The image of the water protector and the slogan "Water is Life!" are catalysts of this generation's climate justice movement. Both are political positions grounded in decolonization—a project that isn't *exclusively* about the Indigenous. Anyone who walked through the gates of prayer camps at Standing Rock, regardless of whether they were Indigenous or not, became a water protector. Each carried the embers of that revolutionary potential back to their home communities. Water protectors were on the frontlines of distributing mutual aid to communities in need throughout the pandemic. Water protectors were in the streets of Seattle, Portland, Minneapolis, Albuquerque, and many other cities in the summer of 2020 as police stations burned and monuments to genocide collapsed. The state responds to water protectors—those who care for and defend life—with an endless barrage of batons, felonies, shackles, and chemical weapons. If they weren't before, our eyes are now open: the police and the military, driven by settler and imperialist rage, are holding back the climate justice movement.

"New Deals"

The Green New Deal (GND), which looks and sounds like ecosocialism, offers a real chance at galvanizing popular support for both. While anticapitalist in spirit and paying lip service to decolonization, it must go further—and so too must the movements that support it.

That's why The Red Nation initiated the Red Deal in 2019, focusing on Indigenous treaty rights, land restoration, sovereignty, self-determination, decolonization, and liberation. We don't envision it

as a counterprogram to the GND, but rather going beyond it. It is "red" because it prioritizes Indigenous liberation and a revolutionary left position. As we show in the following pages, this platform isn't just for Indigenous people.

The GND has the potential to connect every social justice struggle—free housing, free health care, free education, green jobs—to climate change. Likewise, the Red Deal places anticapitalism and decolonization as central to each social justice struggle, as well as climate change. The necessity of such a program is grounded in both the history and future of this land, and it entails the radical transformation of all social relations between humans and the Earth.

We should be mindful of the pitfalls of "new deals." The "deal" in US president Franklin Delano Roosevelt's (FDR) New Deal was, after all, between Northern industrialists and Southern racists to save capitalism from itself during the Great Depression. It was hardly a people's "deal," though it benefited workers and provided necessary relief. For Indigenous people came an "Indian New Deal" as it was known, which itself had mixed results. It brought jobs to the reservations that never had them, improved infrastructure or built it where it was absent, and, in one instance, partially restored buffalo herds that had been annihilated by the military and hunters a generation ago.

The Indian New Deal's hallmark legislation, the 1934 Indian Reorganization Act, ended allotment and repealed a ban on dancing and spiritual practices. It also provided the means to create federally recognized tribal councils, which, in some cases, replaced customary governments. "The Sioux had climbed from absolute deprivation to mere poverty," Hunkpapa intellectual Vine Deloria Jr. said, describing the changes for his people, "and it was the best time the reservation ever had."[3]

Elsewhere it was an engineered nightmare. In the Navajo Nation, Indian agents slaughtered more than half the reservation's livestock. This included about half a million sheep that provided not only income and food, but which had also been integrated as a central facet of the Diné culture and worldview. It was a top-down environmental conservation plan that came directly from Washington, DC, with the logic that settlers can manage Native lands and lives better than Native people. This is a historic issue with conservation movements in this country.

In 1933, FDR authorized the National Industrial Recovery Act, and with it an Army Corps of Engineers project to construct the Fort Peck Dam on the Missouri River, providing employment for ten thousand white workers to pull Montana's economy out of the gutter. Hailed as a beacon of progress and a savior of the region, hydroelectricity was the era's shimmering "renewable energy." The largest dam on Earth at the time of its completion, Fort Peck removed 350 Dakota, Nakota, and Assiniboine families from the Fort Peck Indian Reservation. *Life's* first-ever cover story featured a photo spread of the dam's transient work camp, capturing the rugged ethos of the time. One photo depicted a well-dressed white woman taking a shot of liquor at a bar. Above her hung a portrait of FDR captioned "A GALLANT LEADER" next to a sign that read "NO BEER SOLD TO INDIANS." The photo captures the racial apartheid system—in public places of leisure, work, and everyday life—Indian reservations kept in place at the time.

Fort Peck's success galvanized widespread support for the 1944 Pick-Sloan Plan, which aimed to provide postwar employment by authorizing the Army Corps of Engineers to construct five earthen-rolled hydroelectric dams on the Missouri River. To make way for the dams, an entire river ecosystem was destroyed, and more than a thousand Native families were removed. In the Fort Berthold reservation, four-fifths of the tribe was removed, and 94 percent of their

agricultural lands were flooded. In Lakota and Dakota communities, 75 percent of the indigenous plant and wildlife was destroyed; 90 percent of commercial timber was lost; and one-third of the reservation-based populations were removed—all for hydroelectric power in far-off cities, irrigation for settler farmers, and flood control for downriver states. It was a convergence of the military-industrial complex—a re-colonization of Native lands and waters by a branch of the military through near-wartime levels of economic and political mobilization.

But Pick-Sloan didn't happen in a vacuum; it was part of a broader national energy infrastructure development plan. In the 1930s, the Bonneville, John Day, and Dalles dams on the Columbia River flooded Nez Perce, Umatilla, Yakama, and Warm Springs lands. In 1965, the Kinzua Dam in New York forcibly dislocated more than 600 Seneca. And, an "energy sacrifice zone," the Nixon-era term coined by the National Academy of Sciences, described the Shoshone and Paiute lands taken for nuclear testing at the Nevada Test Site, a 1,360-square-mile "reservation" that was bombed 928 times—nearly half the world's nuclear explosions.

The world-ending atomic bomb was created in secret atop a sacred Tewa Pueblo mesa at Los Alamos National Laboratory in New Mexico. It was tested on Native lands, and the United States became the first and only nation to drop the bomb. The horrors of Nagasaki and Hiroshima were a warning to the rest of world: fall in line, or else. Scientists who maintain the Doomsday Clock set its hands at one minute and forty seconds to midnight in 2020, the closest humanity has been to global catastrophe since the clock's creation in 1947. The two main factors contributing to this threat, experts warn, are global warming and nuclear risk. The atomic age and climate change were made possible by settler colonialism and Indigenous genocide.

The spirit of these times frequently gets forgotten: freedom for some is unfreedom for others. The legacy of the New Deal—which required the plundering of Indigenous lands to keep a settler economy afloat—cannot be the plan for the rest of the planet. Nations of the Global South cannot follow the same path of development as the North in their pursuit of climate equity because the atmosphere has become colonized, disallowing the path for industrialization and development the Global North has followed. The unequal distribution of power—and suffering—is literally in the molecules we breathe and drink. The burden of transition lies at the feet of those most responsible for carbon emission-driven climate change, not those most imperiled by it. The energy consumption of the Global North—especially in the United States and Europe—has to be radically curtailed, not subsidized by more "green" energy. The amounts of resource extraction to facilitate this transition, such as the acquisition of lithium for rechargeable batteries, will come at the expense of other nations who have been historically denied the technology to develop their own resources for the benefit of their own people. The United States, more than any other country, owes a huge share of the climate debt that should be paid—which should be taken from the massive surplus of resources used to militarize the planet and stockpile nuclear weapons—to help nations of the Global South develop sustainably and according to their own values and processes.

Decolonization

In this era of catastrophic climate change, why is it easier for some to imagine the end of fossil fuels than settler colonialism? To imagine green economies, carbon-free wind and solar energy, and electric, bullet-train utopias but not the return of Indigenous lands? Why is it

easier to imagine the end of the world—a zombie apocalypse—than the end of capitalism? It's not an either/or scenario. Ending settler colonialism and capitalism *and* returning Indigenous lands are all possible—and necessary.

The question of restoring Indigenous land to Indigenous people is thoroughly political, which means the theft of it was—and is—not inevitable or beyond our current capacities to resolve. The same goes for Black reparations, ending the hardening of the US border, defunding US imperialism, and stopping the continued exploitation of resources and labor in the Global South by countries up north. "The issue is that accumulation-based societies don't like the answers we come up with because they are not quick technological fixes, they are not easy," Michi Saagiig Nichnaabeg scholar Leanne Betasamosake Simpson has said.[4]

Fifty years ago, decolonization—nations freeing themselves from colonial rule—and land reform inspired global visions for a socialist future, advancing the class struggle further than it has ever gone before by raising the living standards of billions in the Global South. Some Western socialists seem to have abandoned that future in favor of technological pipe dreams like mining asteroids, gene editing, and synthetic meat, without addressing the real problem of overconsumption in the Global North, which is directly enabled by the dispossession of Indigenous and Black life and imperial wars in the Global South. We need a revolution of values that recenters relationships to one another and the Earth over profits.

Anti-Imperialism

The geopolitical relationship countries like the United States have with the rest of the world is deeply intertwined with settler colonialism. Imperial projects build upon settler colonial ones. For the

last twenty years, we've seen the United States destroy countries and communities in a quest for oil. The invasion of Iraq in 2003 was for oil. Cultural treasures from one of the oldest civilizations on the planet were destroyed in the first days of the invasion, but the US military and its mercenary contractors chose to guard oil infrastructure. US oil companies secured contracts with the provisional government the US installed after it deposed Saddam Hussein and the Baath Party. Those who recognized the US' geopolitical motivation for the war soon called for "energy independence" in the United States instead of anti-imperialism. Consequently, Republicans and Democrats spent much of the 2000s promoting oil and gas expansion in the United States and Canada, and this has translated into new oil and gas production on stolen Indigenous lands.

Former US Presidents George W. Bush and Barack Obama supported fossil fuels as the best path towards energy independence, which was also heralded as a means to achieve economic stability and improve homeland security. Both presidents cracked down on nations that strayed from the dictates of US hegemony. In 2002, Bush sponsored a coup d'état against Venezuela's democratically elected president Hugo Chávez, who came to power on a promise to nationalize the corrupt oil sector to fund national infrastructure and poverty relief programs for the poor. When Obama assumed office in January 2009, he continued Bush's sanctions against Venezuela and other nations deemed hostile to US interests. Obama considered natural gas fracking an alternative to coal and oil and he challenged China's subsidies to its national solar industry that would lower the cost of solar production across the world. Like the dams that pulled the nation out of the Great Depression of the 1930s, fracking rigs pulled the nation out of the great recession of 2008. Obama was an imperialist first, a supporter of green energy second.

Increasingly, there is a direct link to the ongoing Venezuelan crisis and oil production in North America. When global oil prices began to fall due to the North American oil boom, a crisis ensued in Venezuela, and the money used to fund the social progress of the country's poorest was all but halted. Around the time that Obama-era pro-oil-and-gas energy policies began to take hold in 2008, during the Great Recession, global oil prices rapidly fell. This was partially due to the United States and Canada building new carbon infrastructure to drill and transport oil from production to market. This oil boom has wreaked havoc on Indigenous nations, with the creation of oil pipelines, the tar sands "dead zones," fracking rigs, and refineries, locking in settler economies to drill at the expense of Indigenous lands and lives. Meanwhile, the boom weaned the US economy from oil imported from countries like Venezuela, whose major buyer was the United States. But the alternative source of oil is much worse.

Both the United States and Canada drilled their economies out of the gutter by producing the dirtiest oil in the world from tar sands and fracking rigs either on Indigenous treaty lands or next door to Indigenous communities. Each subsequent proposal for new carbon infrastructure, like oil pipelines, not only deepens the climate crisis and locks in carbon consumption, it aims to crush Venezuela. Why target Venezuela? It partially has to do with its oil reserves. But it also has to do with the threat it poses as an economic and social alternative to neoliberal capitalism. Venezuelans brought the Bolivarian Revolution into power, which, in turn, increased the participation in social, economic, and political life of Indigenous peoples, women, LGBTQ2+ people, Black communities, and poor people. The nation's oil wealth was redistributed to the lowest sectors of society. And while, for a moment, the US-backed

coup to oust the democratically elected president of Venezuela, Nicolás Maduro, seemed imminent, people took to the streets and to the countryside to defend these hard-fought gains. The Bolivarian Revolution represents a possible alternative to neoliberal capitalism. That's why from its inception it has drawn the ire of Washington, DC. And the most recent standoffs against the construction of oil pipelines at Standing Rock, Bayou Bridge, Line 3, and Unist'ot'en Camp show that the United States and Canada still need to plunder Indigenous lands to make a profit and to keep their economies afloat. Indigenous resistance in North America is at the forefront of combating imperialist plunder, and our struggles are interconnected with our relatives of the Global South.

Venezuela's solidarity has extended beyond its borders to Indigenous nations of Turtle Island, or North America. In 2007, Tim Giago, a preeminent Oglala Lakota journalist, applauded Hugo Chávez and the Bolivarian Revolution for providing heating assistance to hard-hit Indian reservations, the poorest places in North America on the Northern Plains, during the harsh winter months.[5] Citgo Petroleum, a Venezuelan state-owned oil company, had for years donated millions of dollars of heating oil not only to reservations' communities in the United States, but also to low-income Black and Chicanx neighborhoods and homeless shelters.

Prominent Ojibwe activist from White Earth, Winona LaDuke, has also made the connection between the war on Indigenous nations in Turtle Island and the economic war waged against Venezuela. In 2016, during the Dakota Access Pipeline (DAPL) protests, she told *Democracy Now!* that the construction of DAPL "has to do with crushing Venezuela, because Venezuela has the largest oil reserves in the world."[6] It also has to do with crushing one of Cuba's major trading partners—Venezuela.

Cutting off Venezuelan oil to Cuba is part of a US-led blockade against the island nation that has lasted for more than six decades and which the UN General Assembly annually votes to end. The Mas family, an infamous billionaire Cuban-American clan, is responsible for many of the subversive and legislative attacks on Cuba, and much of its accumulated wealth comes from fossil fuels. The family patriarch, Jorge Mas Canosa, founded the Cuban American National Foundation (CANF) and MasTec, one of the largest self-described Latino businesses in the United States that specializes in energy, utilities, and communications infrastructure. In 2017, MasTec's profits rose sharply by 90 percent, due to a high demand for oil pipelines and its role in building a major section of the DAPL, which trespassed through Oceti Sakowin treaty lands. The goal is not only to profit from the destruction of Indigenous lands but also to crush the political alternatives to neoliberal capitalism that Cuba and Venezuela represent.[7]

When looking to the left governments of the Global South, we have to understand that the extractivism of the North is fundamentally based on the imperialist domination of markets, people, and territory. US-backed economic sanctions impact nearly one-third of humanity in some thirty countries, causing untold death and devastation by denying people access to global markets. This restricts a country's ability to generate wealth, stabilize currency, and provide basic human essentials for its people. Countries like Iran, Venezuela, and Bolivia have chosen the path of resource nationalism—that is, nationalizing and developing their own resources for the benefit of their own people and as a mechanism of protection and strength against the predation of the United States and Canada, whose notorious multination fossil fuel and mining companies salivate with each new coup attempt. The price these nations pay for choosing self-determination—delinking from the imperialist supply chain—is

heavy sanctioning from the US that targets their civilian populations with hunger and deprivation.

Sanctions, which are war by other means, had already deprived nations of medical supplies, thus undermining their efforts to save lives from a global pandemic. In March 2020, the UN Secretary-General called for a "global ceasefire" because "the fury of the [Corona]virus illustrates the folly of war."[8] How can there be a ceasefire when sanctions continue to tear through one-third of humanity faster than the pandemic? Coronavirus has shown us that US imperialism holds the world back from responding to pandemics. And as we have seen with the targeting of nations who chart an alternative path, it also holds back the rest of the world from developing alternative forms of energy and sustainability. In other words, because of US intervention, economies of the Global South are not allowed to develop to a point where they can transition away from fossil fuels. Therefore, any climate policy must also be anti-imperialist, demanding an immediate end to genocidal sanctions and the payment of northern climate debt to the rest of the world.

The Red Deal

Some advocates of the GND propose implementing a 70 percent tax hike on the wealthiest Americans to pay for necessary changes. Others argue that seizing the assets of fossil fuel companies, and reallocating money and resources away from state institutions directly contributing to climate change and social inequality must also be part of the agenda.[9] We agree with these proposals, but we understand more must be done. Inspired by the appeals to divest from the financial institutions funding oil pipelines during the Standing Rock uprising and the Movement for Black Lives' divest-invest strategy,

the Red Deal also targets the institutions of the military, police, and prisons for divestment. Imagine divesting from these institutions and opening up $1 trillion to accomplish the task of saving this Earth for everyone.

In 2018, Winona LaDuke pushed for an Indigenous-led GND. The former Green Party vice-presidential candidate inspired us to think about how divesting from fossil fuel infrastructure—such as billion-dollar oil pipelines—could be reinvested into building wind and solar farms and sustainable agriculture on reservations. Indeed, the most radical appraisals of the GND come from Indigenous people. According to the Indigenous Environmental Network (IEN), the GND, as is, "will leave incentives by industries and governments to continue causing harms to Indigenous communities."[10] Before endorsing the GND, IEN called for a clear commitment to keep fossil fuels in the ground; reject carbon pricing schemes; strengthen language on Indigenous peoples and uphold Indigenous rights; and stop, not prolong, our current exploitative and abusive economic and political systems.

A complete moratorium on *all* new fossil fuel extraction—a long-standing demand by Indigenous environmental organizations to "keep it in the ground"—would cause a ruling-class rebellion.[11] Warming temperatures demonstrate how deeply entrenched CO_2 emissions are within class society. Framing this as a panhuman problem or a problem of the species—such as the term "the Anthropocene," the geological age of the fossil fuel economy—misses the point. A select few are hoarding the life rafts while also shooting holes in a sinking ship. Class hatred is warranted. The immiseration of billions sustains the gilded lives of the few. The upper one-tenth of humanity is responsible for half of the carbon emissions from consumption. Half of humanity only accounts for one-tenth of

emissions. The richest 1 percent similarly emit 175 times more CO_2 than the poorest Hondurans, Mozambicans, or Rwandans. Twenty-six billionaires hoard half the world's social wealth, and the world's 2,153 billionaires possess more social wealth than the 4.6 billion people who make up 60 percent of planet's population—numbers that appear to get more extreme as CO_2 concentrations rise. We have to draw lines of separation between us and them, because they have already done so. The 100 companies responsible for 70 percent of global emissions—those relentlessly searching for new hydrocarbon frontiers, market-driven fixes that won't cost as much, or green energy booms—aren't going to put themselves out of business. Nor will the ruling elite put their own system up for debate.

The recent flurry of anti-protest laws from state to state suggests the ruling class is already rebelling.[12] This is familiar: Indigenous peoples pose a radical threat—and pay a disproportionate price—to the fossil fuel industry at the site of extraction and transportation, yet their demands are marginalized within mainstream environmentalism, a trend that has crept into the growing climate justice movement.

It makes sense to expect an Indigenous plan for movement-building like the Red Deal that explicitly names climate change as its impetus to advocate for an environmental justice framework. And, in many ways, we do. We certainly draw from, study, and participate in the pantheon of fierce Indigenous environmental justice efforts that have carried the movement for Indigenous liberation forward throughout these long years of struggle. However, we find that much of what gets framed through an environmental lens—including the efforts to stop pipelines in Wet'suwet'en and Standing Rock—often misses the point about capitalism (and, sometimes, about Indigenous sovereignty too). Conservation and related notions of protection, preservation, and defense—all popular terms in Indigenous

land-based movements like efforts to "protect the sacred"—continue to dominate the framing of Indigenous liberation struggles as efforts for environmental justice. The notion of protecting land and water requires an understanding of what we are protecting it from.

In mainstream conservation discourse, the "thing" environmental advocates protect the land and water from is, typically, capitalist development, which includes infrastructure to expand extractive industries or real estate ventures that include the construction of massive suburbs or housing projects. While the focus is rightly placed on that which we are protecting and defending, what if the question all water protectors and land defenders asked was, why don't we just overturn the system that makes development a threat in the first place? This system, again, is capitalism. Rather than taking an explicitly conservationist approach, the Red Deal instead proposes a comprehensive, full-scale assault on capitalism, using Indigenous knowledge and tried-and-true methods of mass mobilization as its ammunition. In this way, it addresses what are commonly thought of as single issues like the protection of sacred sites—which often manifest in specific uprisings or insurrections—as structural in nature, which therefore require a structural (i.e., non-reformist reform) response that has the abolition of capitalism via revolution as its central goal.

We must be straightforward about what is necessary. If we want to survive, there are no incremental or "non-disruptive" ways to reduce emissions. Reconciliation with the ruling classes is out of the question. Market-based solutions must be abandoned. We have until 2050 to reach net-zero carbon emissions. That's it. Thirty years. The struggle for a carbon-free future can either lead to revolutionary transformation or much worse than what Marx and Engels imagined in 1848, when they forewarned that "the common ruin of the contending classes" was a likely scenario if the capitalist class was

not overthrown. The common ruin of entire peoples, species, land-scapes, grasslands, waterways, oceans, and forests—which has been well underway for centuries—has intensified more in the last three decades than in all of human existence.

Austerity is enforced scarcity. The neoliberal policy of the last forty years has been a tax strike of the super wealthy, who have refused to pay their share of taxes and have locked away the world's wealth in tax havens and offshore accounts. These are resources that should go towards providing services—education, housing, healthcare, public transportation, infrastructure, and environmental restoration—to those who actually produce the wealth: the Indigenous, Black, mi-grants, women, and children who are the workers of the world. This strike is worth crushing quickly and with prejudice. Direct action alone won't reallocate wealth if it is not backed by popular mass movements and enforced by state apparatuses wrested away from the elite and powerful.

Prison abolition and an end to border imperialism are key aspects of the Red Deal, for good reason. The GND calls for the creation of millions of "green" jobs, as well as a policy of "just transition" for poor and working-class families and communities that currently de-pend on resource extraction for basic income and needs, and which will suffer greatly when the extractive industry is shut down. In the United States today, however, about seventy million people—nearly one-third of adults—have some kind of arrest or conviction—wheth-er or not they've served time—that prevents them from holding certain kinds of jobs. If we add this number of people to the approx-imately eight million undocumented migrants, the sum is about half the US workforce, two-thirds of whom are not white. *Half* of the workforce faces employment discrimination because of mass crimi-nalization and incarceration.

The terrorization of Black, Indigenous, Brown, migrant, and poor communities by border enforcement agencies and the police drives down wages and disciplines poor people—whether or not they are working—by keeping them in a state of perpetual uncertainty and precarity. As extreme weather and imperialist interventions continue to fuel migration, especially from Central America, the policies of punishment—such as walls, detention camps, and increased border security—continue to feed capital with cheap, throwaway lives. The question of citizenship—colonizing settler nations have no right to say who does and doesn't belong—is something that will have to be thoroughly challenged as a "legal" privilege to life chances. Equitable access to employment and social care must break down imperial borders, not reproduce them. We address this in more depth in Part II.

A Caretaking Economy

A new green economy is the antithesis of what currently exists: a militarized extractive economy, what Lakotas call *"owasicu owe,"* the fat-taker, the colonizer, the capitalist economy; or what activist Winona LaDuke calls *"Weitiko"*—the cannibal economy. If prisons, police, and the military are the caretakers of violence and agents of death, then educators, healthcare workers, counselors, water protectors, and land defenders are caretakers of peace and agents of life. A green economy should be born from, and center the labor and needs of, caretakers. Indigenous people, for example, are already working "green jobs," they're just not getting paid or enjoying the protections employment offers for land, water, and treaty defense. Caretaking is often unrecognized work that is heavily gendered, severely criminalized, and never fairly compensated. The pay gaps between carceral

and military workers (mostly men), and care workers (mostly women), makes this crystal clear. The climate justice movement needs to center the labor struggle of caretakers if it is to be successful. Caretakers can be powerful authors of a new economic system to replace capitalism through a caretaking economy.

This caretaking economy is already in place. Three-quarters of land-based environments and two-thirds of marine environments have been affected by capitalist development, but environmental degradation has been less severe in places managed by Indigenous peoples and local communities.[13] While making up only 5 percent of the world's population, Indigenous peoples protect 80 percent of the planet's biodiversity.[14] Indigenous peoples and local communities who have distinct cultural and social ties to ancestral homelands and bioregions still caretake at least a quarter of the world's land. This includes places that are the lungs of the world, such as the Amazon rainforest, and its veins, like the Missouri River Basin—areas facing existential threats of deforestation, damming, water contamination, oil and gas development, and mining. Indigenous people protect the land, air, and water we all need to live.

In the United States, Indigenous caretakers have been the most confrontational arm of the environmental movement by blocking the construction of extractive infrastructure. They have therefore also been the most heavily targeted and criminalized. Following the Standing Rock protests, eight states passed American Legislative Exchange Council (ALEC)–inspired "critical infrastructure" laws criminalizing the protesting of oil pipelines. Legislation pushed by the Trump administration would make "inhibiting the operation" of an oil pipeline, such as simply standing in the way of construction, an offense punishable by twenty years in prison. Water protectors and land defenders are the new generation of political prisoners.[15]

South Dakota's "Next Generation Model" legislation, which was drafted by Republican governor Kristi Noem in collaboration with the Keystone XL parent-company TC Energy Corporation, goes beyond the ALEC model. Although overturned, it attempted to create new civil penalties for "riot boosting," which include anyone who "directs, advises, encourages, or solicits other persons participating in the riot." The goal is simple: chill resistance by criminalizing Lakota Water Protectors fighting an oil pipeline trespassing through their treaty territory. The intense criminalization of caretaking reveals the extent to which the ruling class will go to protect its interests and keep capitalism in place. If we're going to have a chance at defeating the fossil fuel industry and preserving the Earth, which keeps us alive, the decriminalization of caretakers and caretaking labor—Indigenous caretakers, in particular—must be a fundamental priority.

Demilitarization

The only reference to national security in the current GND calls climate change "a threat multiplier." The Pentagon used the same language in a 2015 congressional report detailing how all strategic commands are, as a matter of necessity, integrating climate change into their global counterinsurgency operations.[16] The intelligence community's 2019 "Worldwide Threat Assessment" warns that environmental degradation and climate change "are likely to fuel competition for resources, economic distress, and social discontent" in the present and near future by "threatening infrastructure, health, and water and food security."[17]

According to a June 2019 intelligence briefing former US President Donald Trump tried to suppress, the State Department cautions that,

because of climate change, "local problems" in Sub-Saharan Africa, the Middle East, and Central and Southeast Asia make these regions especially vulnerable for unrest that "could spill over with global consequences."[18] The goal, then, is to contain the "threat multiplier": twenty-two million potential climate refugees. The military, which has long produced reports about climate impacts, is already "going green" by focusing on national security, which means protecting the welfare of wealthy countries (specifically US citizens) and their economic interests while portraying those in poor countries, who suffer the worst effects of warming temperatures, as security threats. Most GND advocates to date support security-friendly climate policies.

The Green Party's 2012 version of the GND platform envisioned cutting the bloated US military budget in half—which would still make US military spending the highest in the world and nearly twice as much as China's.[19] The US military, with nearly 800 bases worldwide in more than seventy countries and territories, plays no positive role in the world. Even at half its capacity, the US militarization of the globe has to end. We can start by defunding the US military and reallocating its resources to the parts of the world and the peoples the United States has destroyed, destabilized, or dispossessed. We can also reject the militarization of Global North humanitarianism, which, under neoliberalism, has simply become a mechanism of hybrid war that functions alongside sanctions and warfare to uphold US imperialism throughout the world. We instead advocate for internationalism—the making of just and peaceful relations with the nations of this world—which is based in solidarity that transcends borders and decenters the imperial core.

Land Back

The best forms of environmental policy come from the bottom up, and momentous change only happens with the might of a peoples' movement behind it. In North America, change begins with the land—one of the primary sources of both wealth and inequality. As Dina Gilio-Whitaker from the Colville Confederated Tribes argues in her book, *As Long as Grass Grows*, settler state conservation policies stem from "protecting" slivers of nature by killing and removing Indigenous peoples from the land to create nature reserves, national and state parks, and "public lands." Under Trump's administration, millions of acres of this land were opened to oil and gas extraction, threatening Indigenous sacred sites and surrounding communities.

But private landownership has been equally devastating. The Homestead Act of 1862 carved up 270 million acres of Indigenous territory for white settlers. The invaders pulverized buffalo skulls into fertilizer for their plots—the sacred animals slaughtered by the millions to near extinction to starve Indigenous peoples off the land. Once cleared and settled, homesteading produced wealth for generations of white settlers, while Black, Native, and non-white people were categorically excluded. Where there weren't crops, industrial feedlots and grazing pastures for cattle replaced open-range buffalo herds. Today's large-scale industrial farming raises ethical questions not about how these animals die but about how they live.

Today, white settlers own 96 percent of all agricultural lands and 98 percent of privately owned land in the United States. In 1970, Vine Deloria Jr. candidly spelled out the problem and even suggested a solution to North American settlers: "It just seems to a lot of Indians that this continent was a lot better off when we were running

it," he wrote in *The New York Times*.[20] Perhaps liberal-minded readers of that era thought it was clever wordplay, the posturing of a Red Power militant—attention-grabbing sloganeering, but not a serious political demand. To the original people of this land, it was truth and prophecy: no society can ever have an ethical relationship to a place it stole. And today, Deloria's words sound more like rational environmental policy than militant jargon when compared to what's been on offer: a "drive it like you stole it" mentality or, more accurately, a "live on it like you stole it" attitude.

Under current US law, Indigenous sovereignty provides limited recourse. Tribes themselves represent a third sovereignty next to states and federal authorities. The imperialist foundation of federal Indian law, however, severely limits the exercise of tribal self-government. Racist and colonial legal doctrines that make up the foundation of federal Indian law—such as the Doctrine of Discovery, domestic dependent nation status, and plenary power—and oversight by the Bureau of Indian Affairs, reveal that Indigenous-US relations are colonial to the core and remain centered on the acquisition of land. The successive stages of federal Indian law—allotment, citizenship, tribal enrollment, termination, and self-determination (our current era)—have also, in various ways, presented colonial domination as a form of empowerment, to enable Indigenous consent for their own dispossession. In the 1970s, for example, the Nixon administration reversed the trend of terminating the federal status of tribes by introducing a new direction of "Indian self-determination." Despite the name change, Indigenous peoples and lands today are no more "self-determined" than they were during prior eras, largely because the United States still holds imperial and colonial control over Indigenous nations. (American Indian nations are also the only human beings who are under the boot of the Department of the

Interior, the federal agency in charge of managing wildlife, parks, and Indians). Federal Indian law is due for a complete overhaul—if not total dismantlement—which would go a long way towards undoing the hegemony of colonial relations that keeps Indigenous life and land under permanent siege.

Indigenous laws and governance systems would reemerge in place of federal Indian law. Treaties would be enforced, not by the US government, but by Indigenous nations. Land back would become mandatory, ushering in a different type of development and reconstruction of our fundamental relationship to land not premised on ownership but on collective well-being. Transforming our relationship with the land would create conditions for caretakers (who aren't exclusively Indigenous) to inherit the Earth; to work with, take care of, restore, and heal the land as diverse workers whose labor is bound, quite literally, with the land itself. We are citizens of a land that has yet to be brought into existence, but nonetheless exists in the recesses of our long historical memories and revolutionary imagination.

The focus, however, is not just on land within what is the "domestic" territory of the United States. Demilitarization also means land back to the nations and territories occupied by one of more than 800 overseas US military bases that violate sovereignty and deny self-determination to millions: Guantanamo Bay, Okinawa, Korea, Guam, Hawai'i, the Philippines, Iraq, Egypt, Afghanistan, Puerto Rico, El Salvador, Honduras, Panama, and so many other places the US occupies. Land back means the return of just relations between the human world and the other-than-human world. It means removing the overseas US military threat that encircles and bullies other nations. Land back is about justice and about bringing in a new world based on peace and cooperation, not coercion and force.

It's Not Just an "Indian Problem"

While Indigenous people are framed as the age-old "Indian problem," decolonization and land back aren't *just* an Indian problem. If every struggle were made into a climate struggle—which must be done if we are to have a future on this planet—then every struggle in North America must be made into a struggle for decolonization. The solutions offered in *The Red Deal* must entail a revolution that turns back the forces of destruction. It must penetrate the economic and cultural realms with equal urgency and force. Indigenous peoples should be empowered to develop and implement restorative practices according to their own customs and traditions. Caretakers should not hesitate to take the reins of leadership. The energies and passions of Indigenous peoples at the forefront of resisting extractive capitalism should inspire everyone, as water protectors and land defenders have inspired a generation of climate justice revolutionaries. Indigenous demands for the restoration of land, air, and water are essential for the return of our collective humanity. This is the vision and the mandate of the Red Deal: uniting Indigenous and non-Indigenous people in a common struggle to save the Earth.

Indigenous political structures and economic systems do not apply only to Indigenous people. Our liberation is bound to the liberation of all humans and the planet. What we seek is a world premised on Indigenous *values* of interspecies responsibility and balance. We seek to uplift knowledges, technologies, governance structures, and economic strategies that will make these values possible, in the immediate future and in the long term, and which always have the future health of the land at the center of their design and implementation, Indigenous or not. In this sense, decolonization is for, and benefits, everyone. It also needs our collective cooperation to succeed.

The Four Principles

What follows is a plan of collective climate action based on four principles that we developed after extensive conversation, dialogue, and feedback from Indigenous and non-Indigenous community members, comrades, relatives, and fellow travelers. The first Red Deal coalition meeting was held on June 19, 2019 at the Larry Casuse Freedom Center in Albuquerque, New Mexico. Since then, the platform has been revised and adopted by social movements, politicians, and organizations like the Democratic Socialists of America.

This book is an extension of these original principles, and a reflection on the changing material conditions we confront and how these conditions shape and inspire the vision we set forth in the original document. The Red Deal is a living document in the sense that it should not be taken as gospel, nor as an idealistic or utopian program for change. As conditions shift, so must we. We must be both optimistic and action-oriented—permanent builders. A great deal has changed since we came together in the spring of 2019 to begin our initial discussions about what would later become the Red Deal. The ideas, principles, and plans of action contained within this book have therefore been forged through movement, struggle, and direct action. Some of them have already been tested and revised, awaiting new tests and new potential revisions by those who are moved to take it up within their own struggles and movements. While there is an inherent flexibility built into the Red Deal, we remain steadfast in the following four methods and principles of organizing that anchor the original pamphlet. We encourage you to act upon what you find in *The Red Deal* by applying these principles to your local, tribal, or regional situation.

1. What Creates Crisis Cannot Solve It

Divestment was a popular strategy during the #NoDAPL uprising in 2016. Water protectors called upon the masses to divest from the financial institutions subsidizing the pipeline. *The Red Deal* continues this call for divestment from fossil fuel industries, but we go one step further. We draw from Black abolitionist traditions to call for divestment from carceral institutions like police, prisons, the military, and border imperialism in addition to divestment from fossil fuels.

Divestment is only half of the equation. What will we do with the resources that will become available once we divest from these institutions and practices? As of 2015, military spending accounted for upwards of 54 percent of all discretionary spending at the federal level. Proposed discretionary spending for national security in 2020 comes in at $750 billion, with $718.3 billion slated specifically for the US military. In a given year, the US provides $3.8 billion in military aid to Israel. $182 billion is spent each year on cops and prisons. These figures don't even include revenues from the fossil fuel industry.

Compare this to the $68 billion allocated for education in 2016 and $186 billion allocated for mental health services in 2014. $66 billion of discretionary funding is spent on healthcare each year, with only $5.4 billion allocated to Indian Health Service (IHS), the branch of the Department of Health and Human Services responsible for providing direct medical and public health services to members of federally recognized tribes. Despite treaty and federal obligations to provide adequate healthcare, Native people—especially those living in urban locations—have the worst healthcare in the nation.

Almost half of Americans cannot afford basic procedures and pharmaceutical corporations control these already deficient public services through lobbying. The US government is threatening to further cut spending on education, healthcare, food stamps, and other crucial health and human services in order to inflate military spending, bail out banks, and subsidize fossil fuel corporations. Meanwhile, schools, nursing homes, domestic violence shelters, homeless shelters, soup kitchens, art programs, museums, clinics, public bus lines, community farms, and local businesses are having to raise money through GoFundMe campaigns and bake sales to remain in operation.

Imagine if the US military had to hold a bake sale to keep its doors open while life-giving and sustaining programs were fully funded and never in fear of disappearing. Imagine if we had over a trillion dollars to invest in healthcare for everyone; to increase teachers' wages so they can provide quality free education to everyone; to repair roads and provide safe and accessible public transportation for workers; to provide safe and comfortable homes for elders; and to fund large-scale language revitalization programs in every Indigenous nation on the continent.

While ludicrous under our current system, imagine the world we can build through divestment. With the resources we gain from divesting from the US military alone, we could end child hunger, homelessness, and fund renewable energy on a global scale tomorrow. Literally. There is not, as the ruling class wants us to believe, a scarcity of resources. There are plenty of resources to fund these programs and restore dignity to our relatives; we must simply wrest them from the greedy clutches of the ruling class and redistribute them to the people.

2. Change from Below and to the Left

Anti-protest laws have been considered in dozens of states in the wake of Black Lives Matter and #NoDAPL. At the same time, politicians continue to withdraw from social justice demands for healthcare, housing, and education in the GND, choosing to focus on reforms limited to climate change only. It is important to remember that the GND was possible only because its main proponent, Alexandria Ocasio-Cortez, became politicized by the #NoDAPL uprising. Indigenous people are, and have always been, at the forefront of the struggle for climate justice.

We will not back down from the GND's demands for a dignified life, nor will we back down from centering the leadership of Indigenous people in this fight. In fact, we must go further. We must throw the full weight of *people power* behind these demands for a dignified life. People power is the organized force of the masses—a movement to reclaim our humanity and rightful relations with the Earth. People power will not only topple empire, but it will build a new world from the ashes; a world where many worlds fit.

There can be no rich people without poor people; the rich depend upon the poor. But the poor don't need the rich, we only need each other. This is the power of the masses. Although Indigenous peoples live in a capitalist society, we continue to practice people power. Pueblo communities feed friends and relatives on many ceremonial occasions throughout the year. The original purpose of this was to pry surplus from those who held more wealth and redistribute

it amongst those who didn't so that neither a poor class nor a ruling class could form. Everyone's material needs were met; there was no starvation, no homelessness, no alienation. Everyone was a relative, and everyone had relatives. Capitalism destroyed this world. We must destroy capitalism to bring it back.

People power is the most direct form of democracy. Everyday people decide what's best for themselves, not the elite and powerful. The wealthiest in the world have refused to pay taxes for more than a century while Indigenous people starve and die of preventable diseases. We are of the conviction that crying on the shoulder of the man who stole your land is the opposite of people power. You can't smudge the murder out of capitalism, nor can you expect the powerful to give up their wealth out of the kindness of their hearts. So how do we get things to change? Lobby Congress and politicians? No. We reach out directly to our people, hitting the streets and galvanizing the support of poor and working-class communities. Once community support is galvanized, politicians will follow. Even if they don't, we will continue to organize and build power from below that cannot be ignored nor crushed. Our leverage is people. Leverage comes from a movement behind you, and power comes from reclaiming your rightful path towards equal development. Only when people move do we build enough power to force concessions and, eventually, win.

3. Politicians Can't Do What Only Mass Movements Do

Politicians use the term "reform" as a catchall for their plans for social change. Reform typically means asking the powerful to implement gradual changes that we hope will eventually improve our lives. This approach attempts to treat the symptoms of a crisis, rather than the structures of power that create crisis in the first place. For example, in March 2016 white police officer Austin Shipley murdered twenty-seven-year-old Navajo mother Loreal Tsingine, in broad daylight in Winslow, Arizona. The murder was captured on his mandatory lapel camera—a result of police reforms. Lapel cameras are often cited by police reformers as a necessary deterrent to police violence and killing. Yet Shipley murdered Tsingine with impunity and faced no charges.

The same year Tsingine was murdered, police arrested over eight hundred water protectors and brutalized and traumatized countless others at Standing Rock. That year, police killed Native people at higher rates than any other group, and killed Native women at six times the rate of white women. Yet, when proponents call for reform for Missing and Murdered Indigenous Women and Girls and Two Spirits (MMIWG2S), the solution is often more police.

In 2018 and 2019, we saw an increase in deaths of Indigenous children in migrant detention centers along the US-Mexico border. We witnessed the shooting by US Border Patrol of Claudia Patricia Gómez González, an Indigenous woman from Guatemala. And, we mourned the death of Indigenous transwoman Roxana Hernández in a detention facility operated by US Immigration and Customs Enforcement

(ICE). Immigration reformers have called for Border Patrol to keep families together and have also filed lawsuits to call for the construction of "more humane" cages for these families and individuals.

The question these reformers ask is: How can we improve the police? Who do we need to lobby to make these improvements? Instead, we ask: Why do we need police? Why do we need borders? "*Chinga La Migra*," "Abolish ICE," and "No Ban on Stolen Land" are not mere slogans but demands for a dignified life. The police, military, and Border Patrol exist to protect the interests and wealth of the elite. Instead of providing life-saving housing, healthcare, and food, reforms give us more cops, more soldiers, and more cages.

States protect capital and its caretakers: the ruling class. They do not protect the people. Reformists who appeal to the state for change compromise our future by aligning with the interests of the ruling class. We refuse to compromise. But we do believe in reform—just a different kind, a non-reformist reform that doesn't limit the possibility of what the status quo offers, but which fundamentally challenges the existing structure of power by prioritizing, organizing, and elevating the needs and demands of the masses. We don't want to improve the system by implementing policies from the top down, we want to destroy it—either by fire or a million small cuts—in order to replace it.

Our philosophy of reform is thus to reallocate social wealth back to those who actually produce it: workers, the poor, Indigenous peoples, women, migrants, caretakers of the land, and the land itself. The restoration of social wealth means the empowerment of those who have been dispossessed. Social

wealth can be restored by building a mass movement that has the power and leverage to reclaim resources from the ruling class and redistribute them to the dispossessed.

4. From Theory to Action

From the White House to CEOs of multinational corporations, bosses run the world and plunder without challenge. Given the staggering amount of destruction and death just a few individuals inflict on billions, it is strange that no unified left has emerged in the Global North to pose a real threat to the bosses. We have witnessed in the last handful of years massive grassroots rebellions against the fossil fuel industry, police violence, racist immigration policies, and labor exploitation, yet nothing has coalesced into a unified mass movement. We believe that struggling for non-reformist reforms to restore the health of our bodies and the Earth will serve as the most powerful vehicle for building a mass movement—fast—that can take on the bosses. But we cannot simply be against something—we must be for something.

We will construct our own policies out of grassroots action that seeks to caretake and support one another. Through organizing around non-reformist reforms for housing, food security and sovereignty, domestic and gender violence justice, suicide prevention, land restoration, and more, we can and will build infrastructures of liberation. As the Black Panther Party decided at a certain juncture in its history, The Red Nation realizes we must undertake realistic and principled actions now that will help build our cumulative capacity

for revolution in the future. We must not turn away from the truth: we do not yet possess the capacity for revolution, otherwise we would have seen a unified mass movement come out of the remarkable revolutionary energy of the past decade. And yet, we have very little time to get there. This is the contradiction and the duty of our generation: decolonization or extinction.

While the idealism of the left is a stunning beacon for the world we seek to live in, ideas alone will not save us. As we say in our Principles of Unity, "We can die having had the 'correct positions' but having accomplished nothing and freed no one." We must build the world we seek through building power. We build power by building movements, and we build movements through coming together with other working-class people. Correct ideas and theories of change that are worthy of reproduction only matter if they arise from, and directly nourish, our collective movements. We must build our people's confidence to theorize and respond to material conditions, assess the tools and means of struggle available to us, and act upon this knowledge.

We worry that what is currently on offer from the left, however important and well-intended, is not enough. We cannot simply heal our individual trauma, nor can we consume better to save the environment. We cannot vote harder, nor can we place all our hope in a few individuals in Congress. We cannot bounce from insurrection to insurrection, nor can we continue to funnel our energies into nonprofit organizations. We cannot build isolated utopias while the rest of the world burns, nor can we spend our time debating one another online. Climate change will kill us before any of these actions

liberate the planet from capitalism, let alone improve our lives enough to wage a successful revolution.

Liberation isn't a theory, it's a necessity and a right that belongs to the humble people of the Earth. How will we make it happen? We will not turn away from opportunities to organize, agitate, and build people power in spaces of state surveillance like prisons, child services, hospitals, and classrooms that are designed to dehumanize and disempower the people. The state sets its targets on poor and working-class people because it knows they pose the greatest threat to its existence. We will not let the state steal our relatives or gut our power any longer. We must swarm the state, inside and out, multiplying the threat by millions until it crumbles.

Indigenous people know that every moment of our existence is mediated by the state—it is fundamentally violent and rigged in favor of murderous elites. We have no wish to reform or perfect it. But we refuse to relinquish the power of state institutions—the sheer resources available to humanity—to the ruling class. To do so means we cede key terrain to fascists who set fire to our future and reformers who water down our demands and kill us by a million small cuts. We must wield people power in all arenas to build our movement, we must create the conditions for liberation by any means necessary. We will not be fooled by reformist doublespeak, nor will we relent in our plans for liberation, whatever strategy we choose. We will operate from a position of strength that holds the abolition of capitalism and total liberation as its uncompromising core.

Our non-reformist reforms will come in many forms. They will look like grassroots Indigenous seed bank networks

where thousands of sustainable farmers share, trade, and feed their communities. They will look like successful runs for city council elections where left candidates implement a people's platform for climate and social justice at city and municipal levels. They will look like land back camps or tribal council resolutions that reject colonial water settlements by banding with other Indigenous nations to blockade all government and corporate efforts to commodify water. Whatever form they take, we must simply get to work.

This book comprises three areas of struggle—Divest, Heal Our Bodies, Heal Our Planet—and a conclusion. In each area, we discuss critical caretaking concerns. It is not enough to simply provide criticism; radical critique must caretake the collective relations of liberation to actualize it. The first section calls for ending occupation and draws inspiration from the history of Black liberation struggles and the platform of the Movement for Black Lives that calls for the abolition of, and divestment from, the prison industrial complex. We also connect with struggles against militarization and colonial occupation. The second section elaborates how a reinvestment strategy should center around common humanity and a social justice approach. Divestment from occupation and prisons requires a reinvestment in collective practices for healing our bodies. The third section advocates for a reinvestment strategy in a common future for the entire planet. The massive amounts of resources dedicated to the military and prison industrial complex should be reinvested and reallocated towards paying climate debt to the rest of the world and to helping to heal the ravages of capitalism and imperialism. The conclusion is a call to action; to step into the strong current of history that is the tradition of Indigenous resistance.

DIVEST

End the Occupation

Capitalism requires a powerful military industry for its processes of accumulation and imposition of control over territories and natural resources, suppressing the resistance of the peoples. It is an imperialist system of colonization of the planet.
—People's Agreement, 2010

Introduction

The occupation of Indigenous land and settler colonialism has yet to end. Despite historical narratives of progress in the United States, colonization is not a thing of the past. It is what shapes our present. Roxanne Dunbar-Ortiz writes in *An Indigenous People's History of the United States*, "To say that the United States is a colonialist settler-state is not to make an accusation but rather to face historical reality, without which consideration not much of US history makes sense, unless Indigenous peoples are erased."[1] Settler colonialism is an ongoing project of erasure of Indigenous peoples in order to replace them with settlers, who claim to own and dominate the land. The occupation of this land has always been maintained by violence or by the threat of violence. The US invests billions of dollars in its tools of occupation: the military it uses to enforce its global domination and steal natural resources from the Global South; the police it empowers to repress domestic resistance to occupation; and the prisons it funds to warehouse and punish those who do not adhere to settler capitalist social norms.

These three institutions have coalesced into the military and prison industrial complex (MPIC), an occupying force on stolen land that operates by reinforcing settler dominance, white supremacy, and global imperialism. The military and prison industrial complex refers to the concentration of government spending into private interests for some perceived social good that, in reality, supports corrupt industries. The military-industrial complex takes public money to make war profiteers rich, and those private corporations are awarded lucrative government contracts to develop expensive technologies of destruction at the public's expense.

Similarly, mass incarceration has risen in the United States with support of both the Republican and Democratic parties, to create jobs in devastated rural economies and move undesired populations out of cities. It serves as a population release valve for the contridictions of capitalism. Increasingly, private prisons are making money on the incarcartation of Black, Brown, and Indigenous peoples. To date, the United States imprisons more people than any other country in the world.

With funds, equipment, and training from the federal government, police across the US employ armored vehicles, chemical weapons, and military tactics of counterinsurgency to suppress protests. They have exported these tactics, many of which they learned in the genocidal Indian Wars of the nineteenth century, to militaries and police forces of oppressive regimes across the world. Equally concerning, US police and military personnel have been trained by Israeli occupation forces in the most modern techniques and technologies of settler colonialism. On top of this international state violence, oppressed people in the United States face vigilante violence from settlers intent on defending white supremacy along the southern border, in towns surrounding Indigenous nations, and in cities across the country. As we have seen recently with the Black Lives Matter uprisings, the police and military are deeply entwined with white supremacist militias, far-right groups, and fascist formations.

The US MPIC is the greatest purveyor of violence on the planet. Given the immense power and resources that support the settler occupation of Indigenous land and global imperialism, we must find effective ways to diminish and defund these institutions. Without confronting the structures that murder, displace, imprison, and oppress us, we will not be able to create alternative ways of being, as these will be swiftly targeted and crushed as threats to the existing status quo.

Divestment is a strategy for dismantling these structures. At its most basic, divestment is the removal of funds, resources, and energy from what harms us. It has a long history in powerful movements against injustice, including: the global movement to end apartheid in South Africa; the Boycott, Divest, and Sanctions movement to end Israel's occupation of Palestine; and the fossil fuel divestment delegations Indigenous women led as part of the #NoDAPL movement in 2016. The US Border Patrol employs Israeli technology developed for the walls of Gaza and the West Bank, and US police departments send officers to learn tactics of repression from Israel's occupation forces. The exchange of technologies of violence must be stopped, for ourselves and for our Palestinian relatives.

We have identified five areas of struggle within the larger MPIC as priorities for large-scale, targeted divestment campaigns.

Area 1: Defund Police, Immigration and Customs Enforcement, Customs and Border Protection, and Child Protective Services

The first area of struggle we see in ending the occupation is defunding the occupational forces that oppress us. The US invests immense resources in policing its subjects, patrolling its borders, and enforcing colonial domination in order to maintain settler control over these lands it occupies. Rather than addressing the structural causes of poverty, displacement, and colonization, the state criminalizes Indigenous and other colonized people. The police in particular have historically brutalized oppressed communities and operate as an occupying force in poor communities. They serve the interests of the settler ruling class by protecting private property, evicting people from their homes, and, as we have seen with the various uprisings

in the history of the US, crushing any resistance to colonial occupation and racism. Today's police are well versed in military tactics and counterinsurgency, which they deploy on water protectors, land defenders, protestors against the murder of unarmed Black people, and anyone who defies the ruling class.

Xenophobia against people of color is a staple of white supremacy in the United States. Since the creation of the Customs and Border Patrol (CBP) and Immigration and Customs Enforcement (ICE) in 2003 in the wake of 9/11, the police have increased cooperation with federal agents to capture, incarcerate, and deport migrants from Asia, Africa, and Latin America. CPB and ICE were created out of the Patriot Act as part of the "War on Terror." This war targeted Muslims in the United States and abroad. The reforms gave ICE agents unprecedented powers to harass US citizens, often people of color traveling on public transit. Agents have carried out many murders, sexual assaults, and human rights abuses while patrolling the southern borders and detaining migrants. Obama expanded the war to targeted assisnations with drone strikes, including the assassination of US citizens abroad without due process. Obama earned the name "deporter in chief" for ramping up immigrant deportations. In 2016, Trump expanded on Obama's deportation infrastructure and began a policy of family separation that imprisoned migrant children and parents in detention centers and in county jails.

An example of state violence is Child Protective Services and its removal of Indigenous children from their families and tribes. Throughout the long and ongoing history of Indigenous genocide, one of the tactics of settler society is the removal of Indigenous children. From the late nineteenth century until as recently as 1973, Native children were taken away to boarding schools to be stripped of their identity and assimilated into settler society, which falls under the *UN*

Convention on The Prevention and Punishment of the Crime of Genocide, "forcibly transferring children of the group to another group."[2] Today, Native children are taken away by Child Protective Services at disproportionate rates and families are separated due to poverty and criminalization. Since 1978, the Indian Child Welfare Act (ICWA) gave tribes some protections from child removal by requiring that Native children removed from their families be placed with other family members, a family within their tribe, or an Indigenous family of another tribe before being adopted by white families. However, the ICWA has come under legal attack. In 2013, in *Adoptive Couple v. Baby Girl*, the US Supreme Court started to whittle away at the protections in the law, denying a Cherokee father custody of a child his white wife put up for adoption after separating from the father.

Altogether, the police, immigration agencies, and Child Protective Services use immense resources to discipline, exclude, and disrupt Indigenous people along with everyone targeted by state violence. We seek to defund these institutions first. Ending the occupation means taking away the power of the state to oppress us. There are many ongoing campaigns to defund municipal police so that cities can spend their money on other projects that will actually benefit the masses and we encourage you to join them. With the 2020 uprisings against police murders, calls for disbanding and abolishing police, ICE, and CBP have coalesced into a coordinated movement led by Black and Indigenous organizations, trans rights and feminist groups, and advocates for incarcerated people. Support your local Black Lives Matter organization and the many others who are actively organizing campaigns to reallocate funds. Check if your city has a campaign to stop the deadly exchange or start one yourself.

Coinciding with the struggle to materially weaken police departments, we must also work to fight the glorification of police

benevolence and the idea that "blue lives matter" more than ours. We must refuse the cooptation of our movements through reformist calls for community control or diversity hiring of police officers. Since the Civil Rights Movement, the police have recruited from minority communities to induce us to brutalize our own people, yet we have seen no material improvement to our treatment by the police. This speaks to the trap of seeking representation within oppressive systems: having cops who look like us will not change the underlying relationships of violence that maintain the status quo. This is partly due to the power of the police unions, which serve to shield police officers from accountability and which do not, like labor unions, serve the needs of workers. Instead, police unions protect the violent defenders of private property and white supremacy.

We must also turn our attention to the violence that is occurring along the US-Mexico border, both in the deserts where agents and vigilantes chase and murder asylum seekers and in the detention centers imprisoning those fleeing violence and economic despair. We urge you to join efforts to close the detention centers and to release all migrants and the reunification of families. If you are able, you can organize your communities into networks of support for migrants and asylum seekers and provide material support, shelter, legal representation, and deportation defense. We must fight for the freedom of all migrants, without exceptions or "good immigrant" narratives that would exclude some and ultimately justify the criminalization of all.

The police and border patrol tactics and technologies we are facing here are very much connected to global patterns of war, occupation, and border enforcement. We draw your attention to the collaboration between US police agencies and the Israeli occupation forces that displace, harass, and murder Palestinians in their homelands.

Ultimately, we must take our communities' safety into our own hands since we know that the settler state will not protect us and will only harm us in its efforts to maintain dominance. We have seen the rise of community self-defense such as that of the Black Panthers, the Brown Berets, and the Indigenous communities that have faced off with the Klan and colonial military in the US and Canada. One tactic that we have seen used successfully is what is known as "cop watch," where community members observe and record interactions between police and people in their neighborhood. It is legal to film police in most cities as long as you are in a public space and maintain enough distance. In fact, many of the cases of police brutality that have sparked the global Black Lives Matter movement and recent calls for police abolition did so because they were recorded. While many people film arrests and other interactions with police, it is important to focus cop watching on the police themselves and care should be taken to not endanger or incriminate the targets of police harassment. For this reason, it is often paired with know-your-rights trainings and pamphlets that can be given to community members who witness the arrests and harassment by police, explaining to them why you are filming the police and how they can protect their community from police brutality.

Finally, the police cannot be the solution to the problems our communities face. Taking inspriration from the Missing and Murdered Indigenous Women, Girls, and Two Spirits (MMIWG2S) movement, which demands the investigation and prevention of violence against Indigenous women, girls, and two-spirited peoples, we must not rely on the police. Rather than relying on police and increasing their funding and power to investigate crimes against Indigenous people that the police themselves often commit, we should organize community defense initiatives against violence. Part of the problem of protecting

ourselves from settler state violence is that many Native people find themselves away from their communities or in bordertowns, where tribes have little to no jurisdiction or power.

Area 2: End Bordertown Violence

Bordertowns emerged from the dispossession, relocation, and ethnic cleansing of Indigenous people. Borders manifest themselves outside of the common understanding of national boundaries marked by fences, walls, and checkpoints. They are also found within the settler nation itself, at the boundaries between Indigenous and settler communities.

Bordertowns are those that surround Indigenous nations, often with significant populations of Native people, yet they are typically marked and policed as white spaces; in the same sense that suburbs were originally (and still are) perceived as spaces for whiteness. The function of a bordertown is to exploit the identity, labor, and death of Indigenous people. Indeed, often a bordertown's economy relies on Native workers and white tourism to museums and stores that contain our art, ceremonial objects, and even the remains of our ancestors. On one hand, settler occupation is always built on Indigenous death, and on the other, bordertowns trade in a narrative of an Indigenous "past" for tourism.

Territories held by Indigenous nations came under settler control during the several centuries of European settlement and westward expansion through war, massacre, treaty negotiation, and privatization followed by forced selling, all of which forced Indigenous peoples off their homelands and onto reservations. The Homestead Act of 1862 and Dawes Act of 1887 served to divide entire nations into individual landholdings that, coupled with threats of violence and

increased dependency on the European capitalist economy, could be transferred to private settler ownership. Many Indigenous people were forced to sell their parcels of land in order to settle debts, pay taxes, or feed themselves and their families.

The Homestead Act gave large tracts of these lands as well as those recently secured by US Army violence to white settlers for very cheap and was repealed only in 1975, after transferring millions of acres of land to white settlers. As Indigenous nations became dislocated from their lands and forms of subsistence, they increasingly became forced into wage labor for the very settlers who stole their land. They also were forced to rely on nearby trading posts and mercantile stores to exchange rug weavings, pottery, and wool for everyday necessities. Settlers, on the other hand, were largely dependent on Indigenous labor in the early years of westward expansion and, to this day, bordertowns rely on Indigenous people to work, shop, and create products to sell in stores or markets that profit off of Native art and culture.

Many of these lenders, pawnshops, and trading posts offer Indigenous people a small profit for family heirlooms or artwork while selling these items at a higher price to white collectors, museums, and wealthy individuals. Car dealerships, payday lenders, and other predatory businesses prey on Indigenous people on and off reservations by locking them in an endless cycle of debt. This relationship of capitalist exploitation in bordertowns continues the long history of colonial extraction from Indigenous peoples, lands, and labor. These bordertowns, like those along the southern border, are locations of extreme levels of surveillance, policing, and violence in order to contain the "threat" of Indigenous existence that contradicts the myth of settler society. The continued presence of Native people signifies the incompleteness of the settler project, which responds

with anti-Indigenous violence. Violent interactions with the police are common, along with the enforcement of laws restricting Native peoples' movement and behavior that proliferated as bordertowns arose across the West.

In many cities, laws prohibited Indigenous people from living within the city limits unless they were servants to wealthy whites who agreed to house them on their property, out of sight. While these laws have since been repealed or evolved into anti-vagrancy laws that criminalize homelessness, panhandling, and even resting in public, bordertowns have a long history of violent anti-Indian sentiment. A common form of violence inflicted upon Indigenous people is "Indian rolling," or the targeted assault, torture, and murder of Native people. The term was first used in 1974 to describe a gang of white teenagers' murder of three unsheltered Diné men in the bordertown of Farmington, New Mexico. The history of anti-Indian violence is, of course, much older than this.

In addition to the state violence enacted by the US military during the Indian Wars, private settlers, militias, and companies engaged in decades of unilateral violence against Indigenous people. State and federal governments paid these settlers for their service in volunteer militias that hunted, killed, and captured Indigenous people throughout the western states. They collected bounties for scalps and body parts and often took it upon themselves to organize and arm these militias to wage genocide against Native people.

This anti-Indian violence has evolved over the centuries into the forms of bordertown violence we face today. For example, "Indian rolling" is an ongoing issue in bordertowns, where mostly white and Hispanic teenagers and men target Native people because of these deep, underlying logics of anti-Indianism. In 2014, three Hispanic teenagers attacked three Diné men in Albuquerque, New Mexico and

bludgeoned two of them to death while one narrowly escaped. The three teenagers expressed no remorse and were described by the media as unmotivated by racial hate, yet as we have seen, they were practicing a long American tradition of anti-Indian violence.

This violence also takes on a particular gendered form in bordertowns, especially in areas where resource extraction occurs. Indigenous women, nonmen, and trans and nonbinary people experience higher rates of violence—more than any other race—inflicted by white supremacy and heteropatriarchy. MMIWG2S, which will be described more thoroughly in Part II: Heal Our Bodies, is rarely framed as a form of bordertown violence and both are described as recent phenomena.

Gendered violence and anti-Indian violence have long upheld the colonial project of resource exploitation, relocation, displacement, and genocide since the first military outposts and forts were constructed along the western "frontier" of the fledgling United States. Native women and girls were lured, sold, and kidnapped to be sex trafficked to soldiers and traders who manned these outposts and forts, and the same happens today in settler cities. Bordertowns are the original "man camps," where men who work in extractive industries live while on the job in oil and gas, logging, and mining. One of the first lines of struggle to end bordertown violence is the MMIWG2S campaign.

Another front line against bordertown violence that needs urgent attention is unsheltered Native populations who face a large portion of settler violence, both state and private, yet rarely receive justice when they are targeted by police, Indian rollers, white supremacists, or white business owners. Unsheltered Indigenous people are criminalized for merely existing and are constantly forced to move from place to place to avoid arrest and harassment. White business owners

respond violently to unsheltered Native people because of their disruption to the capitalist economy and to the image of bordertowns as tourist traps selling Native cultural items as trinkets. Therefore, we must move to organize unsheltered relatives into communities capable of defending themselves from settler violence and to directly advocate for their safety and well-being. Tent cities, which are autonomous communities of unsheltered people with communal services and their own forms of governance, have been successful in providing unsheltered people with safety in numbers, access to food, medical attention, and supplies, as well as a sense of community rather than social isolation. We call on everyone to defend tent cities from the frequent police raids and sweeps that have destroyed tent cities across the country.

We also believe that the formation of tent cities should be politicized against settler colonial violence, creating spaces explicitly open to unsheltered Native people who have been displaced from their homelands. We must ensure our unsheltered relatives are involved in the organizing we do for climate and economic justice, housing for all, healthcare, and anything that will impact them. Similarly, we urge everyone to organize with unsheltered people against anti-poor and anti-homeless laws like trespassing, restrictions on panhandling, sleeping in public, and others that criminalize poverty and homelessness. These local laws have spread to cities with significant unsheltered populations, criminalizing and displacing people rather than addressing the underlying problems of settler capitalism. There are many ongoing campaigns to repeal or prevent these laws from passing, often led by unsheltered advocacy groups. If there aren't any yet, we encourage local groups to initiate them. It is critical to protect unsheltered relatives in bordertowns where anti-Indian logic marks many for death.

One of the obstacles preventing Native people from being protected in settler society is the limitations imposed on tribal sovereignty. In 1978 the Supreme Court ruled in *Oliphant v. Suquamish Indian Tribe* that Indigenous nations could not prosecute non-Natives for crimes they committed on reservation lands or against tribal citizens off-reservation. They based this ruling on conclusions that "Congress' actions during the nineteenth century reflected that body's belief that Indian tribes do not have inherent criminal jurisdiction over non-Indians,"[3] which was of course during the Indian Wars and genocidal militia incursions throughout the West. A later case ruled that tribes could not try members of other tribes until an act of Congress made it so that tribal nations could prosecute other Native people, but not white settlers. This double standard demonstrates the racist notions of white superiority enforced by the courts.

The result of this limitation on jurisdiction has been the relative powerlessness for tribes and tribal members to seek justice for crimes committed against them by settlers on and off reservation lands. Particularly in crimes related to sexual and gender violence, this limitation contributes to the continued colonial and patriarchal violence inflicted on Native communities and is part of the reason why sexual assault perpetrated by non-Natives is so common for Native women. Man camps, Christian missions, trading posts, and bordertowns are all sites where settlers interact with Native peoples without accountability. This extends to violence against Native peoples in bordertowns whose cases are not pursued by settler courts and are beyond the jurisdiction of their own tribes' courts. For this reason, we encourage tribal citizens to lobby their tribal governments to enforce treaty rights that follow tribal citizens rather than being tied to a particular geographical location,

as they currently are. Just as American citizens' rights follow them even when they enter and commit crimes in tribal communities, treaty rights should follow Native people wherever they go, even off-reservation.

When Native peoples have been attacked or murdered in border-towns by settlers there has been no recourse for tribal governments except to publish statements condemning the attacks and asking settler courts to prosecute the cases. Treaty rights, as agreements between sovereign nations, must be extended to our relatives off-reservation in order to protect them from the violence of border-towns. One action that we have seen done successfully in police and prison abolition, campaigns against fossil fuel corporations, and in human rights efforts globally is the People's Tribunal. Rather than taking our complaints to the settler courts that deny Native people's sovereignty and other colonized peoples' humanity, a People's Tribunal puts judgment and justice in the hands of the people. For example, when companies have polluted communities through industrial waste but have not been held accountable by the state, people have organized to express their own verdict on corporations that harm them and declare what action will be necessary to remedy those harms. While normally symbolic and educational in nature, the People's Tribunal can carry out investigations into police and vigilante violence, discrimination, and exploitation that occurs in a community, hear testimony from witnesses and victims, and present recommendations to local governments for changes that the people identify are necessary. They are public gatherings that can develop in our communities a sense of control over our own safety, especially in hostile bordertowns intent on erasing Native people.

Area 3: Abolish Incarceration (Prisons, Juvenile Detention Facilities, Jails, Border Security)

Incarceration is not an Indigenous practice. The idea of locking people up as punishment was brought to Turtle Island with the European settlers who colonized it. In Europe they had established debtor prisons to punish those who could not survive within the emerging capitalist economy or to persecute religious minorities in dungeons. In America, prisons and incarceration have historical ties to racialized slavery. Chattel slavery—owning people as property—required extreme forms of violence, fear, and discipline to maintain. African and Indigenous people who were enslaved to work on plantations resisted in many ways, including escape. Settlers formed slave patrols and militias to hunt Indigenous people that later evolved into the current institutions of the police and military we face today.

Prisons and jails in particular have a deep connection to racialized slavery. Even after it was abolished, former plantations were converted into prison work camps where Black people, arrested for any number of minor "crimes" laid out by racist laws, were forced back into slave labor. The Thirteenth Amendment, which outlaws slavery except as punishment for a crime, actually expanded the available forced labor to include poor people even if they were not Black. Prisons and jails today serve to remove people from our communities, breaking up families and disrupting kinship, while either forcing them to work or labeling them unemployable if they are charged with felonies. Incarceration in the United States has proliferated over the past decades to levels unseen anywhere in the world. In fact, while it has only 5 percent of the world's population, the US holds 20 percent of the world's prisoners. There are over two million people who have been incarcerated in their lifetimes and when we include people on

parole, probation, in jails and prisons, one in every thirty-five people (seven million total) in the US are currently under state surveillance or direct control.

Over ninety thousand youth under the age of eighteen are incarcerated in either juvenile detention centers or, if tried as adults, in adult facilities. This mass incarceration is of course racialized, with Indigenous people locked up at rates much higher than their proportion of the US population. Incarceration has had direct effects on millions in our communities as well as their families, which often take on the financial burden of supporting their incarcerated family members. Mass incarceration involves massive amounts of money: in tax dollars spent (with an average of $148,000 spent per person incarcerated per year); in the costs paid by inmates who must purchase their own soap, clothes, and other necessary items; as well as by families of inmates who have to travel to remote locations for visits or pay for collect phone and video-chat calls. The interconnected system of laws, prisons, corporations that use cheap labor from inmates, and all of the other institutions profiting from incarceration, is what is known as the Prison Industrial Complex (PIC). The PIC extracts profit from the suffering and bondage of our communities while disrupting our social relations.

More recently we have seen the prison industrial complex expand to lock up migrants with the creation of ICE and CBP in 2003. Under bipartisan federal administrations, immigrant detention and deportation has risen in response to the growing migration of people fleeing neoliberal economic policies and violence in Latin America. City and county jails have turned to incarcerating detained migrants caught on the border or within the country and new migrant detention centers have been built by the federal government in collaboration with private prison companies and even religious institutions

like Baptist Child & Family Services, which operates multiple migrant detention centers in Texas. Trump's family separation policy, initiated in 2017, made it so that all migrant children crossing the border—including those seeking asylum—would be taken from their families and placed in youth detention centers.

It is important to point attention to the vulnerable populations that are targeted and impacted by incarceration. For example, LGBTQ2+ people are disproportionately criminalized and incarcerated, and are often mistreated once inside jails that are organized around strict gender binaries. Many who are incarcerated and excluded from employment are forced onto the streets where they are at even greater risk of police violence and harassment as well as gender and sexual violence. Single mothers and parents of color are also especially vulnerable as incarceration typically leads to loss of employment and very often can result in losing custody of their children while they are incarcerated. We must pay particular attention to the ways that incarceration disrupts our communities' abilities to survive, maintain kinship, and live dignified lives.

With the current dominance of incarceration as a "solution" to settler society's problems, many social services including mental health and drug rehabilitation are administered through carceral institutions. We must begin to create viable alternatives to incarceration that address the needs of our communities. We cannot rely on police who murder us or prisons that dehumanize us to provide the services we need.

Domestic violence support, as well as shelters for Indigenous women, LGBTQ2+ people, and unsheltered people, are areas where we need to build networks of support outside of the carceral state. Because we do not believe that systems created for our enslavement, brutalization, and oppression can be reformed, we invite you to join

struggles for abolition of prisons, jails, juvenile detention centers, and border security agencies and facilities. While calls for abolition have recently increased due to the uprisings against police brutality, abolition has a long history, especially among Black people who resisted enslavement and have led the movement to abolish incarceration. We look to the work of twentieth-century prison abolitionists as well as those who carry on the work today, and we urge you to join or support the work of organizations like INCITE!, Critical Resistance, the Movement for Black Lives, and many others working explicitly towards prison abolition.

Area 4: End Occupation Everywhere

The United States owns the deadliest and most funded military power in the world. It invests more in its military than the next seven largest military powers combined. The US military also owns more international military bases than any other country.

Why does the United States invest so heavily in its military? The answer can be found in the creation of US settler sovereignty, forged through war against Indigenous nations. In its early years of existence, the United States needed free land to repay war debts following its war of independence with Great Britain. Looking westward from its original settler colonies to find this land, it created the first federal administration of Indian affairs office within the Department of War in 1789 to negotiate treaties with Indigenous peoples to take land in "fair trade." However, when Indigenous peoples refused to sell their land, George Washington and the United States were ready to wage war, or in Washington's words, to "extirpate" Indigenous people.

These efforts failed, largely because Indigenous nations were more powerful than the thirteen states at the time. The fledgling

US government waited until another opportunity arose some thirty years later to attack these nations and gain control of their lands. This time it was through legalized theft. The most belligerent of these laws, the Marshall Trilogy (1823–1832), unilaterally changed the status of Native nations from foreign nations—their status according to treaties—to colonized subjects of the United States. Between 1823 and 1832 the US Supreme Court's fourth Chief Justice, John Marshall, as Diné geographer Andrew Curley states, "defined the status and rights of Indigenous nations within the United States as 'tribes,' uncivilized peoples dependent on it and subject to its complete authority."[4] Drawing from the Doctrine of Discovery to justify the domestication of Indigenous nations, the Marshall Trilogy fabricated laws to alienate aboriginal title and strip Indigenous nations of their independence.

The Marshall Trilogy demonstrates how the foreign status of Indigenous nations posed an existential (as well as material) threat to the United States, which had already proven its intentions for vast territorial, political, and economic expansion. As the original foreign nations in the way of US expansion, Indigenous nations thus had to be terminated by any means necessary. Legalized theft was used alongside treaties and military campaigns (which included starvation, imprisonment, massacres, and scorched earth policies) to force termination.[5] Its assault on Indigenous nations shaped the United States' first decades of existence, not only giving birth to what we now know as the United States, but also defining its very existence. Although not thought of as such, the colonization of Indigenous people by the United States was, and continues to be, a project of imperialist invasion.

In her 2007 book *New Indians, Old Wars*, Dakota scholar Elizabeth Cook-Lynn defines US treatment of Indigenous nations as a

quintessential form of imperialism: "a national policy of territorial acquisition through the establishment of economic and political domination of other nations."[6] She notes that wars today are driven by the same "colonial aggression and imperialistic nation building" as the wars of old.[7] "If there is one policy behind the scenes that links the Iraqi experience of the twentieth century to the Lakota/Dakota Sioux experience of the nineteenth," she writes, "it is the policy of imperialist dominance. Trampling on the sovereignty of other nations for most of its several centuries of nationhood has been the legacy of the American Republic's power."[8]

The original imperial violence enacted by the United States through Indigenous genocide and colonization in North America continues to this day, all in the name of natural resources, territorial positioning, and profit. Look at Standing Rock in 2016 when Indigenous people defending their treaty lands against the construction of the Dakota Access Pipeline were brutalized by the National Guard, which was sent in to detain and assault water protectors and land defenders. Look at Hawai'i and Mauna Kea where Kanaka Maoli—Hawai'i's Indigenous people—continually face violence from the US military, along with being arrested by police for protecting their sacred sites. Look at Venezuela, which is under sanctions for refusing to cave to US bullying for oil. Look at Palestine, surrounded by two of the largest US military aid recipients, Israel and Egypt. Look at Okinawa, where in early 2019, tens of thousands of Japanese citizens called for the closure of US military bases. Look at Guam. Look at Vietnam. Look at Bolivia. Look at the Philippines. Look at Afghanistan. Look at Iraq. The Indian Wars never ended; the United States simply fabricated new Indians—new terrorists, insurgents, and enemies—to justify endless wars and endless expansion.

In order for humanity to live free from this violence, we must center the decolonization of Indigenous nations and dismantle all laws, bombs, guns, sanctions, banks, corporations, social customs, and agreements across the globe that perpetuate US imperialism. Only then can we truly achieve liberation and justice for Indigenous nations in Turtle Island and for all oppressed nations across the world living under the boot of US domination. This means that advocates for Indigenous decolonization in the Global North must have strong analyses and an uncompromising stance on US imperialism. Our struggles for sovereignty and self-determination are the oldest anti-imperialist struggles against the United States. We owe it to our kin in the Global South to remember that our struggle for liberation is the same struggle they face.

We must unite against our common enemy. We have much to learn from one another. Our Indigenous relatives and comrades who gathered in the spring of 2010 in Cochabamba, Bolivia to draft the revolutionary climate document, the People's Agreement, remind us that US imperialism does not happen only through laws and warfare. Imperialism wreaks havoc on the world through capitalism. It keeps resources in the hands of a few while the rest of humanity starves and the Earth dies. Drawing upon ecofeminist, ecosocialist, and Indigenous principles and knowledge as tools to combat climate change, the People's Agreement is a pact from the Global South and social movements that centers the needs of the majority of the planet, calling for an end to capitalism rather than maintaining the hyperconsumption of countries like the United States.

Because the burden of US-driven climate change has been externalized to the Global South (and Indigenous people specifically), the People's Agreement makes the case for enforcing climate debt, and names the special responsibility that the United States—among all

other developed countries—has for paying this debt and other reparations for its imperialist violence. Ending the occupation everywhere thus means centering an effective and principled approach to climate change, thereby releasing the burden from Indigenous nations and placing responsibility where it belongs. To this end, we urge people in the United States to organize campaigns that enforce the following demands for developed countries listed in the People's Agreement:

- Restore to developing countries the atmospheric space that is occupied by greenhouse gas emissions. This implies the decolonization of the atmosphere through the reduction and absorption of their emissions.

- Assume the costs of technology transfer needs of developing countries arising from the loss of development opportunities due to living in a restricted atmospheric space.

- Assume responsibility for the hundreds of millions of people that will be forced to migrate due to climate change caused by these countries, and eliminate restrictive immigration policies, offering migrants a decent life with human rights guarantees in their countries.

- Commit to a new annual funding of at least 6 percent of GDP to tackle climate change in developing countries. This funding should be administered free of conditions and should not interfere with the national sovereignty or self-determination of the affected communities and groups.

Organizing to implement these demands can also be viewed as a form of divestment and reinvestment. As the People's Agreement notes, an annual funding pool to repay climate debt that is comprised of 5 percent of the US' GDP is "viable considering that a similar amount

is spent on national defense, and that five times more has been put forth to rescue failing banks and speculators."[9] What if we created a system where the funds spent on imperialism in the form of defense and bank bailouts were redirected to heal the Earth by decolonizing the atmosphere and building a dignified future for our relatives in the Global South? This is not simply a question to ponder. It is a life-or-death program we must take seriously.

The United States is holding the rest of the world hostage, denying dignity to billions of people, and literally killing the Earth. Not to mention that US imperialism makes it impossible for other nations to practice basic self-determination or make any meaningful gains when it comes to climate change without constant interference and aggression from the United States, which usurps and thwarts any efforts it perceives to be against its own selfish interests. Only until we embrace anti-imperialism as the heart of our movements for Indigenous liberation will we be able to call ourselves true relatives—good relatives—to our kin in the Global South. We should start by organizing campaigns and movements to implement the People's Agreement.

Area 5: Abolish Imperial Borders

European colonial powers brought notions of both private property as well as nation-states from Europe to the Americas. One of the first things did was impose borders and national boundaries on the lands they occupied. The Doctrine of Discovery enshrined in the Catholic Church's papal bulls—and still cited by the US Supreme Court—stated that the European power that "discovered" a land had the sole right to purchase or steal land from Indigenous people who lived on it. This exclusion based on colonial occupation and "discovery" was

the basis of European-style sovereignty that divided Indigenous land around the world with borders. Since that time, borders have been used to control and restrict the movement of certain populations of people but free up and allow the movement of capital. The United States recognizes no borders other than its own when it seizes land through violent military force or topples governments of other nations who refuse to bend to the will of its corporations. This is the definition of imperialism, and borders play a key role.

In fact, the first act of US imperialism was its westward expansion from the original boundaries of its thirteen colonies into the territories held by Indigenous people and supposedly protected by treaties. Manifest Destiny, which called for the US to dominate "from sea to shining sea," made Indigenous people the first victims of US imperialism. In 1823 the Monroe Doctrine, a foreign policy tenet upheld by successive US administrations that acts as if the entire Western Hemisphere is the exclusive domain of the United States, exerted its control over Latin America. The US continues its imperial occupation, manipulation, and economic domination of Central and South America and has spread its imperial reach even further around the world with its over 800 known military bases. The US military and capital have no borders; only people of limited means are bound by borders. This merging of borders with nationalism, capitalism, and imperialism requires us to develop a comprehensive analysis of how borders restrict, control, and govern the movement of Indigenous and other racialized people.

The US has restricted migration from its southern border with Mexico since it invaded and declared war during the Texas and California republics when Anglo settlers occupied the future states and requested US military support. This started the US-Mexico War. Following the Mexican Revolution and after Chinese people migrated

through Mexico because of the Chinese Exclusion Act, the US militarized its southern border and the first Border Patrol operations began. It wasn't until the September 11, 2001 attacks that the US had an opportunity to "secure" the nation by clamping down on migration from the southern border with the creation of the Department of Homeland Security (DHS). The national security apparatus, along with the media, have created the narrative of a "border crisis" that has continued to justify inhumane border enforcement in the name of national security. By declaring a crisis and framing caravans of asylum seekers fleeing the effects of US imperialism as an invasion of the nation's borders, the US has been able to mobilize both enormous resources and public support for tighter border controls and violence against migrants along the border.

The border and its violence extend beyond even the physical boundaries of the nation. The US military and police have established surveillance systems and military training programs in other countries in order to prevent migrants from reaching the US. The series of restrictive laws following the September 11, 2001 attacks allowed border enforcement activities like checkpoints and racial profiling further inward from the militarized border zone, within 100 miles of the actual national borders and coasts. Migrants within this internal boundary face widespread surveillance, profiling, exploitation, and the risk of deportation or incarceration every day.

These forms of border imperialism demonstrate how important it is to recognize the regulatory control that borders represent. This control happens through the surveillance of bodies, management of exclusion, and administration of punishment. Borders function as structures of segregation and weapons of empire. Article 13 of the *United Nations Universal Declaration of Human Rights* states the right to freedom of movement as an intrinsic human right.[10] Given

the mass migration of humans and other-than-humans from the Global South to the Global North—which itself is caused by US imperialist-colonialist practices and capitalist-driven climate change—we must open and abolish imperial borders to assist in the free movement of all life.

As the Arab Resource and Organizing Center (AROC) has spelled out, freedom of movement is a fundamental human right. The freedom to stay is the right not to be deported or restricted based on race, ethnicity, or religion. Indigenous people have the right to stay and live in their own homelands. The freedom to move is the right to migrate or move without restriction and threats of violence based on racist, xenophobic immigration policies. Refugees have the right to sanctuary. The freedom to return should be granted to refugees, such as Palestinians, to return to their homelands from which they have been expelled. Families and relatives separated by detention, migration, or relocation have the right to return and be reunited with their loved ones. The freedom to resist any impingement on these fundamental human rights to movement and return is also a fundamental human right.[11] Let us not forget no one is illegal on stolen land except for those who have stolen it.

This is why our most potent challenge to border imperialism is Indigenous sovereignty itself. Multiple Indigenous nations have been bisected by the northern and southern borders and are facing destruction of their territories and ancestral burial sites by the construction of the border wall. In 2020, land defenders of the Kumeyaay and Tohono O'odham Nations have resisted construction of the border wall and have faced violent repression from the police, Border Patrol, National Guard, and the National Park Service. We must support these nations in asserting and defining their sovereignty that exists beyond the boundaries of the US

settler state. We must also work to build relations with Indigenous peoples from the Global South, especially those whose people are migrating to the US due to American economic policy, military intervention, and support of right-wing governments. We should build connections between these nations and Indigenous movements in North America, Oceania, Asia, Africa, and the Middle East so that Indigenous peoples globally can express solidarity in the face of continued anti-Indigenous violence.

Closer to home, we can begin to build upon the tribal sovereignty that our nations have fought for by pushing for sanctuary resolutions in tribal governments that offer migrants protection from deportation, detention, and harassment. This expression of solidarity to our distant kin is also an important assertion of nationhood and sovereignty. The settler state should not be able to dictate who can or cannot remain on land it stole. Indigenous nations must lead the challenge to the very notion of settler control of the land and non-Indigenous relatives and those displaced from their own homelands can reciprocate by acknowledging Indigenous sovereignty. US-dominated global capitalism has created conditions around the world that cause people to be displaced, to flee poverty or violence, and to seek other places to live.

This has been particularly evident with the migration of Africans from across the continent to Europe, which carved up Africa into colonial territories in the Berlin Conference of 1884–1885. By the early twentieth century, Europe controlled the vast majority of Africa and continued until the decolonization struggles of the 1950s and 1960s. Even now, Europe's economic policy and its forcing African nations into debt continues to dominate without being directly in control as it had in the past. Yet, when African people flee the conditions created by European exploitation, they are met with a fortress of border

enforcement, walls, and inhumane apathy towards migrants who have drowned crossing the Mediterranean Sea. We urge everyone to turn their attention to the global nature of migration and particularly its roots in economic policy and military intervention. With the growing threat of climate change causing people to migrate, it is important to note how the US military apparatus is preparing to exclude and contain climate refugees.

Colonial borders impose limits not only on humans but on our other-than-human relatives as well. Many plants and animals inhabit the spaces bisected by the border and their migratory patterns are threatened by the further militarization of the border with the construction of ever-taller walls. In the past, the US has destroyed our animal relatives in the name of imperialism, as when they forced Navajo Nation citizens to reduce the number of sheep grazing on the Nation's land in order to fit within the reduced size of the reservation; or when the US military nearly eradicated the buffalo when they were trying to expand their territories westward and could not defeat the Oceti Sakowin militarily. The southern border now threatens our human and other-than-human relatives that have always migrated freely across these lands before colonization. Therefore, we call for the abolition of border imperialism in our broader movement to end the occupation, because no one is illegal on stolen land.

HEAL OUR BODIES

Reinvest in Our Common Humanity

Introduction

Often, in Indigenous knowledge, we see humans are the youngest species. Because of this, we rely on our older, nonhuman relatives to guide us and give us structure on how to live in a good way. From the plants, rocks, animals, and hydrothermal vents on the seafloor to the arid mountains of colonial Chile, there are countless communities found throughout the Earth, not all of them human, and there are countless relationships that have been gifted to and cared for between these communities. From this relationship with the Earth, the Sun and days, we also see the relationship that we have with the cycles and patterns of our own bodies, the seasons of our flesh. It is from the plants and the animals and the air and the water that we draw our patterns of organization for cultures and societies. Our bodies operate in tandem and in balance with the natural world. This acknowledgment of, respect for, and dedication to the life of things, their rhythm and organization, is how we heal our bodies. This basic assertion has always been the root of Indigenous struggles for life, and it will be the path towards liberation once again.

But today, as we have been for hundreds of years, Indigenous people are profoundly unfree. We are under constant attack by capitalism. Whereas our culture is based on regeneration, capitalism is based on death and seeks to kill all that gives life. Capitalism is an infection that has forced our cells to adapt to its hoarded wealth, quartering of the Earth, and mass depletion of resources. Our lives have been made into numbers and statistics, debt packages, experiments, and commodities. Since the arrival of Europeans, Indigenous nations have struggled fiercely against the project of capitalism. Ours has been a struggle for life. Yet we are constantly delegitimized by policies and reforms that refuse to address the root of the infection causing us to suffer.

Capitalism creates and accumulates wealth based on speculation, or making profit based on changes in the value of goods on the market, and searches constantly for new frontiers of value. Under neoliberalism, capitalism has turned our well-being (and our suffering) into a marketplace where human life is sold, commodified, traded, and consumed. Neoliberal capitalism financializes everything, turning all aspects of life and death into cascading horizons for exploitation and profit in the interests of the ruling class, including the unexpected windfall that COVID-19 has provided for the uber-wealthy, like Jeff Bezos and Elon Musk.

Our suffering is bundled and rebundled as debt for Wall Street speculators to exploit and sell. When we are not being financialized, we are being murdered, caged, and harassed or neglected and abandoned. Sometimes, this happens all at once. Under neoliberal capitalism, everyday people have had to work longer and harder while wages have decreased, benefits have dried up, and state-sponsored support mechanisms have evaporated through privatization and budget slashing.

These conditions led to a decade of massive anti-austerity uprisings in nations like Greece, Lebanon, Chile, France, Ecuador, and the United States. Part of a larger, global movement against social and economic abandonment, these uprisings have held states accountable for policies that shrink public programs for food, housing, education, transportation, and healthcare in the name of "fiscal responsibility," while simultaneously offering subsidies and incentives for multinational corporations to continue plundering the Earth. As they facilitate new forms of capital accumulation for these corporations, neoliberal states throughout the world simultaneously claim to have a scarcity of resources. They peddle this narrative to justify the slashing of social welfare but it is simply false. Why else

would military spending increase during the neoliberal period, or the wealthiest 5 percent of the world's population get even richer?

The anti-austerity movement has forced us to confront a disturbing truth: capitalist states are not concerned with public welfare. Rather, they function as hoarders for the ruling class, which watches with indifference while billions perish. This is apparent in how wealthy nations like the United States have handled the COVID-19 pandemic, encouraging American citizens to identify themselves as consumers who should be shopping around for the best vaccine (to line the pockets of pharmaceutical corporations) rather than looking to the state for assistance or solutions. The US government's response to the pandemic confirms that suffering is the only option on the table when it comes to capitalism. We are consigned to endure ever-expanding deserts of abandonment. Meanwhile, the ruling class consoles everyday people by offering paltry, weak-willed policies to "create jobs" and "stimulate the economy." Such policies and reforms produce almost no change and people are left to sit and fester, watching their relatives barely survive or die. This is what counts for "progress" and "success" in a world controlled by capitalism. As the anti-austerity movement has shown, it is simply too much to bear.

We must therefore develop and fight for alternatives to capitalism, not as an aspiration, but as a matter of urgent survival. This requires an informed, practical, and action-oriented approach. We believe the issues we pinpoint in this chapter are the most important areas of struggle that can wield the greatest and fastest gains toward alleviating our relatives' suffering and building a larger movement to dismantle capitalism. Capitalism will fall—we are certain of this. We can heal our bodies by continuing to hammer cracks into its foundations, eventually pounding it into dust that joins the soil, from which new life can emerge.

Area 1: Citizenship and Equal Rights

There are currently an estimated forty-seven million immigrants within the borders of the United States, of which approximately twelve million are undocumented. War, unequal trade relations, global wage disparities, underdevelopment, and climate change have created the conditions for massive migration from the Global South to the Global North. Migrants from the Global South face treacherous journeys, criminalization and detention, family separation, trafficking, unsafe and underpaid working conditions, murder, and severe restrictions on becoming citizens or legal workers. While progressives, leftists, and radicals in the United States have shown outrage about the flagrant brutality of US immigration policy along the US-Mexico border, there is still a denial of US imperialism in causing migration in the first place. We urge everyone to understand how US imperialism operates.

First, the United States continues to play a pivotal role in causing war and conflicts, and in overthrowing Global South governments in Libya, Syria, Somalia, Afghanistan, Iraq, Nigeria, Honduras, Bolivia, Nicaragua, El Salvador, Haiti, Colombia, and elsewhere. Using hybrid war techniques that combine ideological and military justification for intervention elsewhere in the world, the United States also foments economic and political destabilization, such as by using sanctions and conditional aid in countries that it deems "hostile" to US capitalism. According to the United Nations, neoliberal economic policies are responsible for most of the migration from these areas of the world to the Global North (and to other Global South nations). Austerity in the Global South has made the lives of local peoples so unlivable that they must flee to find sustainable work, healthcare, education, and housing.

Second, the United States has shaped a world economy predicated on free trade agreements that favor the wealthy nations. These agreements open up markets in the Global South to heavily subsidized food commodities from the Global North, causing local farmers to go out of business. Free trade agreements are designed to favor large corporations, including big agribusiness. This puts small farmers througout the world at peril. These trade arrangements pit workers and farmers against each other, leading to declining labor rights, environmental regulations, and commodity markets that are important to small-scale famers like coffee growers.

The North American Free Trade Agreement (NAFTA) of 1994 was an instructive example of the effect of US commodities like industrially farmed corn—which are supported by federal subsidies and price protections—being sold at low prices in Mexico and Central America where subsistence farmers cannot compete. Many of these displaced corn farmers fill the ranks of migrants who have had to either move to urban areas in their home countries or make the passage to the United States. In addition, these agreements open up land and resources for privatized development, causing the displacement of Indigenous populations and leaving environmental catastrophes. Enshrined in these agreements are rules that ensure low wages and global wage disparities, as well as little-to-no protections for the environment. These conditions force many to migrate in search of jobs.

Third, climate change caused by the burning of fossil fuels is also causing desertification, drought, stronger hurricanes, rising sea levels, and increasingly extreme weather patterns. This is exacerbating conflict and forcing migration. The United States has about 5 percent of the world's population but consumes 25 percent of the world's oil. Additionally, the US military is the number-one global consumer of

oil. The United States is also the number-one greenhouse gas emitter on the planet.

Given the damage US imperialism and global capitalism continue to cause throughout the world, our movements for decolonization and liberation must address both directly. We must start by embracing and practicing an internationalist outlook and commitment. Building a mass antiwar and anti-imperialist movement to end war, sanctions, and resource extraction must be the priority of every progressive and left organization regardless of their specific "issue." Strengthening the international labor movement and uniting workers from the imperial core with workers in the Global South must also be a priority and should bring together representatives of workers' movements from around the world. One of the demands of such efforts should be the creation of a global minimum wage to end the global wage disparities. The US and other wealthy nations currently exploit differences in minimum wage and the advantage of currency exchange rates to access cheap labor to manufacture goods and extract resources. Workers of the world should be able make a living wage wherever they are, without having to leave their homelands, and those who do migrate should be afforded livable wages and work conditions.

We must listen to the demands of our relatives from the Global South who argue that citizenship for migrants in receiving countries is a human right. Migrants deserve a decent life with full human rights guarantees conferred by citizenship. This should apply not only to future migrants, but the forty-seven million who currently reside in the United States, regardless of their current legal status. Given the role of US imperialism and its wars, economic hoarding, and mass pollution, US citizenship is not the horizon of what we should be trying to achieve when we call for migrant justice.

Citizenship efforts should pay special attention to climate migrants, who are forced to migrate due to climate change caused by the Global North (and the United States in particular). We must hold the US accountable for driving climate change. We must organize campaigns that force the US to pay reparations for war and climate debt. The US' climate debt, calculated through the amount of carbon emissions released into the atmosphere compared the available "budget" of atmospheric gasses, was estimated in 2015 to be at least $4 trillion.[1] As many nations in the Global South have stated, repaying the debt of colonialism and imperialism in full will be impossible for wealthy nations who refuse to change their relationships to poorer nations. Reparations will ensure that countries in the Global South will be able to develop sustainably and guarantee sustainable livelihoods for their citizens, thereby decreasing emigration and raising the quality of life for all. As a matter of justice and reparations, we must also organize campaigns to eliminate restrictive immigration policies in the US. This should entail shutting down the camps, shutting down all detention facilities, abolishing ICE, ending family separations, and allowing people to migrate freely.

Area 2: Free and Sustainable Housing

Close your eyes, take a breath, and allow yourself to imagine a world where all people enjoy safe, comfortable housing. Imagine a world where no one is poor or hungry, where all families are allowed to stay together and nurture their homes. Imagine a world where having a home does not depend on money or status, but simply on the fact that you are a human being. Imagine a world where everyone has a true *home*; not just a shelter, but a real home filled with love, laughter, food, rest, and joy. Now, open your eyes and look around

at what currently counts as a "home": unsheltered relatives sleeping on sidewalks and under tarps, thousands of families living in cars, urban housing filled with cockroaches and cancer-inducing lead, overcrowded reservation houses with no running water or heat, and rundown apartment complexes that overcharge for rent and exploit tenants.

There is no safety or dignity under capitalism. Not only do most working-class people have no true home, but many do not even have adequate shelter. Millions are one paycheck—and in some cases, less than a week—away from being unsheltered. According to the Department of Housing and Urban Development (HUD), 42,000 to 85,000 Natives would be unsheltered if relatives were unable or unwilling to squeeze multiple families into already over-crowded homes.[2] Furthermore, HUD estimates an approximate total of 68,000 new housing units are needed in tribal areas to combat this invisible housing crisis, a total that matches the more visible ten-year housing plan already in the works for New York City's crisis. While poor, working-class, and unsheltered people are suffering through this housing crisis, a surplus of empty private properties exist across the United States and placement for unsheltered people and families could easily be made—if this was a priority. Housing is inaccessible when profit cannot be made of it. It's clear that we cannot depend on a capitalist system that values profit over people to fix this ongoing crisis.

Much of our attention as leftists and progressives is paid to unsheltered folks, those who live on the streets and are considered "homeless." But is a house without heat, water, or electricity really a "home?" Is a shelter without a functional kitchen or a safe place to sleep really a home? A 2016 article in *The Atlantic* noted that of the 135 million homes in the United States, thirty million are hazardous.[3]

This means thirty million families are regularly and unfairly exposed to health risks like asthma and pneumonia that reduce life expectancy and affect everything from mental health to education. And, although heating and electricity for private residences is the greatest contributor to carbon emissions, the mansions and McMansions belonging to the upper classes are clearly responsible for a large chunk of these emissions. After all, how can reservation or urban dwellings without heat or electricity possibly contribute to carbon emissions?

Our homes are where we live our lives, and perform basic functions like cooking, eating, sleeping, bathing, and making kin. If we consider the unsafe condition of housing/shelter for a large portion of the working class, then the term "homeless" applies to a much larger group of people than those who are unsheltered. We thus propose a program for action that seeks to provide free and sustainable housing for everyone. All people deserve the basic human right of shelter without having to worry about the possibility of displacement, health risks, or danger. We can implement a number of different strategies and campaigns to work towards this goal. We can organize grassroots direct action to place unsheltered people and families in empty surplus housing. In Albuquerque, for example, there are hundreds of vacant single-family homes on the west side of the city that are immediately available for this type of use. The recent campaign known as Moms 4 Housing in Oakland, California, and the efforts to house unsheltered families by occupying vacant buildings it has inspired in other cities, are examples of how direct action led by unsheltered people can confront houselessness. These types of direct action place the right to shelter over the profit motives of the housing market. We can move towards ending private ownership of housing entirely by practicing collective living and building tenant-owned housing cooperatives, where housing is held collectively

rather than being commodified. Indigenous practices of collective land stewardship directly counter the privatization of property that causes poverty, houselessness, and displacement.

Area 3: Free and Accessible Education

A person's access to education is directly related to the condition of their housing. Many Indigenous, Black, and migrant children struggle with academic performance in school because of unstable and hazardous housing. Education is also hindered by lack of access to: adequate and free healthcare; learning tools such as computers, phones, or Internet service; and transportation from home to centers of education. In other words, education is linked to almost every other area of priority we have identified in this chapter.

There is a unique intersection between gender and sexual equality and education. For example, LGBTQ2+ students are more likely to experience violence in schools than other students. Ten percent of all LGBTQ2+ students have reported being threatened with a weapon in school and 34 percent report being bullied in school.[4] Transgender students are especially targeted in schools, with recent rules released by the Department of Education under Trump-appointed Betsy DeVos that discriminate against and exclude trans students by preventing them from reporting harassment, participating in sports, or even using the restroom at school.

As with professions such as healthcare workers, teachers in regions considered "conservative" or "right-wing" have been at the forefront of militant working-class struggle. Education workers are essential workers in a caretaking economy. Teaching is also a highly gendered and undervalued profession. Over 77 percent of all K–12 teachers are women, but they make around 20 percent less than

college-educated workers in other professions. Teachers in West Virginia, which ranks third-to-last in teacher pay compared to other states, organized a wildcat strike in 2018 to protest low pay and the high cost of health insurance. The vast majority of those striking were women.

Indigenous youth receive some of the poorest education. Since the inception of Indian Residential Schools in the US and Canada, for instance, Indigenous children have been stolen from their homes and subjected to physical, verbal, and even sexual abuse to force them to unlearn their languages and cultures and, ultimately, break Indigenous resistance to US dominance. The carceral legacy of boarding schools continues with contemporary child welfare practices that remove Native kids from their homes, adopt them into white families, and strip them of their identities. These practices operate in tandem with school policing and school-to-prison pipelines.

As if this were not enough, graduation rates for Native people are shockingly low. Only 69 percent of Native students in public schools graduate high school. The percentage drops to 53 percent for Native students enrolled in Bureau of Indian Education schools (some of which are boarding schools). Of all Native students, only 17 percent go to college, and only 13 percent have postsecondary degrees.[5] In addition, most K–12 cultural curriculum available for Native students is overseen and decided upon by non-Native school boards.

Often, public schools are funded by revenue generated from anti-Indian economic practices. In New Mexico, for example, K–12 schools and postsecondary institutions are funded by oil and gas revenues that violate Indigenous sacred sites for profit. This means important gains like teacher salary increases and tuition breaks for working-class college students are often made at the expense of Indigenous people. While this scenario may not be true for all

contexts, we cannot ignore the fundamental connections that exist between environmental justice, public education, public health, Indigenous liberation, housing, and labor. We will not be able to attain free education for everyone if we do not simultaneously address these other issues. Free education simply cannot come at the expense of land, water, or Indigenous people.

In addition to organizing campaigns and movements to address the other areas of struggle we identify in this chapter, we should demand that tribal leaders and Native educators be in charge of curriculum for Native students, including delivery in public schools that are not under the control of tribal jurisdictions. Until we can end our dependence on fossil fuels, and as a form of divestment and reinvestment, the revenue made from gas and oil on reservations and sacred sites should be given directly to Native communities to support their students on- and off-reservation. We should organize campaigns in our local school districts for mandatory Indigenous history in all K–12 social studies classes. And finally, we can develop a queer feminist labor platform by collaborating with LGBTQ2+ student groups and organizing with teachers to increase resources and protections.

Area 4: Free and Adequate Healthcare

Under capitalism, a worker's worth is tied directly to their ability to generate profit. Once a body is broken and no longer able to perform labor for ruling class owners, capitalism does not hesitate to cut workers and their families loose from life-saving income and health insurance. But as the West Virginia teacher wildcat strikers pointed out, having "good" health insurance still does not guarantee adequate healthcare, nor is it affordable for the majority of workers who barely make enough after monthly premiums to pay for necessities

like housing, food, education, and transportation. People attempting to use their private- or employer-provided health insurance are routinely met with a web of confusing bureaucracy, hidden charges, denials for necessary procedures, and limited pharmacy formularies. In other words, the current healthcare system in the United States is failing working-class people.

Meanwhile, capitalism dictates every other aspect of healthcare. Pharmaceutical companies drive up prices for essential drugs like insulin, leading to unnatural deaths because people who cannot afford medication attempt to ration (or replace) their drugs in dangerous ways. Driven by greed, doctors receive kickbacks from pharmaceutical companies to overprescribe addictive medications like opioids, which has caused tens of thousands of overdose deaths in the United States alone. An estimated 27.5 million people—8.5 percent of the US population—went without health insurance in 2018, directly contributing to more deaths.[6] And in 2019, fewer than half of American households could afford a $400 health emergency—even if these families had what is considered good health insurance! Almost as many people report that a $1,000 health emergency would put them on the streets and at risk of going hungry. Consider this: the cost of a motorized wheelchair for a person requiring mobility assistance can be anywhere from $15,000 to $30,000, which is equivalent to one year's salary for minimum-wage workers! How are working people supposed to pay for these costs? Many will choose to work instead of seeking care because the costs are so prohibitive. The choice of feeding and clothing their families takes priority. This lowers the quality of life for all and proves that what counts as "healthcare" under capitalism is simply inhumane. We want healthcare that values everyone's life, and we do mean *everyone*.

There are several interrelated areas of healthcare that need our urgent and special attention, including trans health, nutrition, disability, elder care, reproductive health, dental health (which is falsely seen as separate from health insurance), behavioral and mental health, abortion, addiction, and HIV/AIDS treatments. We can address these by organizing direct health services for unsheltered and poor relatives, including: providing regular, free, and nutritious community meals; distributing Narcan to prevent opioid overdoses; offering needle exchanges; handing out free condoms. We can also organize campaigns to help new mothers. A significant portion of childbirth-related deaths happen in the weeks and months after birth, not during the birthing process itself. Contemporary reproductive health practices completely ignore follow-up care for new mothers and mothers are often marginalized in ableist activist culture. We can and should change how we organize for liberation to center mothers, families, and children.

Because they are collective and working class, grassroots organizations often practice lateral caretaking, especially for those who have been abandoned by society because they are poor or considered abnormal. Caretaking often comes in the form of assisting relatives with material needs like food, transportation, housing, and education that they would not receive otherwise. Grassroots organizations are also often safe spaces for relatives who experience social violence in their homes or families.

We encourage people—especially youth—to join grassroots organizing efforts. Organizing with other people creates a social context of accountability and relationality that helps with a number of health-related issues—such as anxiety, stress, and depression related to alienation and isolation under capitalism. Instead of taking our anger out on ourselves or our families, organizing allows us to

channel our feelings into concrete steps that facilitate our liberation. To put it simply: organizing makes you feel good because you are supported and part of a group working towards a common destiny of well-being. Build grassroots organizations!

Area 5: Free, Reliable, and Accessible Public Transportation and Infrastructure

Public transportation is not a funding priority for federal or city governments, despite surveys showing that over 70 percent of people in the United States want better public transportation. In fact, it is often one of the first services that city councils will withdraw funds from to funnel towards other areas. Conversely, law enforcement routinely receives the majority of state and city funds, with almost three times more funding than public transportation and increases each year. In Pennsylvania, for example, funding is actively and intentionally diverted from public transit programs and funneled into police departments. Transit security also commits a significant portion of the overall police violence that Black, Indigenous, and migrant workers experience.[7]

Living near city-run bus stops and major routes can make or break a worker's ability to maintain a job or access health services. Yet, there are obstacles even when public transit is available. Landlords and developers capitalize on transit infrastructure and raise housing prices for properties close to transit and major roadways, treating access to transportation as a luxury rather than a basic human right. While public transit releases fewer emissions per person than private vehicles, it is not accessible to most workers, 10 percent of whom do not have access to a private vehicle. And in many metropolitan areas, less than 50 percent of workplaces are accessible by

public transportation. This percentage shrinks even further when we consider that an "accessible workplace" is one that can be reached within ninety minutes.[8] Who wants to commute ninety minutes for a minimum wage job?

Lack of public transportation and poor road conditions in and around reservations make travel for basic necessities like groceries, healthcare, and school difficult for many Native folks. Road maintenance on reservation roads can be funded up to ten times less per mile ($500) than what is allocated for state and city roads ($5,000). Road conditions are often poor, with over 60 percent of roads unpaved and almost a quarter of bridges deficient, making public transportation a serious public health hazard for Native people. Indigenous nations are often unable to address these conditions because they own and maintain less than 10 percent of reservation roads. The lack of funding for infrastructure within Indigenous nations is an obvious form of abandonment on the part of state actors.

Access to reliable transportation is one of the biggest factors in maintaining or preventing poverty, and even life itself. Organizing for free, reliable, and accessible public transportation and infrastructure must therefore be an area of priority for the left. We must organize campaigns to increase operation hours and routes/areas of service, which in turn would mean more jobs for bus drivers, whose labor struggles should always be connected to movements for free and accessible public transportation. In order to wage successful campaigns, we must realize that of all federal transportation appropriations, 80 percent goes to highways, whereas only 20 percent goes towards transit. The vast majority of these funds line the pockets of private contractors who make a profit from infrastructure projects and automobile corporations who lobby to improve highways so that consumers will continue to purchase and drive private vehicles.

This means that the majority of public money—our money—goes towards inflating the profits of the ruling class. We must advocate for public money to go to operational costs like driver wages, gas, and bus maintenance, which creates stable employment for thousands of working-class people. We can also advocate for city governments to stop paying private corporations with public money and instead funnel federal appropriations into subsidizing transit, so it is free for everyone regardless of income or access to resources.

We should also utilize the present energy behind defunding the police to demand less armed police and security on public transit. We can also advocate for city governments to defund law enforcement more generally and put those funds into better public transit. In addition to these considerations, it is important to understand that transit systems often own a significant portion of land in cities, especially land adjacent to important routes. This land can be used for building affordable homes that are close to these routes rather than being sold and leased to real estate developers for the purposes of gentrification. Combining housing justice with calls for better public transportation in our local organizing can facilitate these connections and strengthen our efforts to support poor and working-class populations in urban areas. Finally, we must acknowledge that the call for better public transportation is also a sovereignty issue because Indigenous nations need jurisdiction over their roads to improve them. We should always advocate in our public transit campaigns for Indigenous people to have complete sovereignty over their lands and infrastructure, including roads, highways, and transportation systems.

Area 6: Noncarceral Mental Health Support and No More Suicides!

Native people in North America have some of the highest rates of suicide not only in the country, but in the world. And we are not alone. LGBTQ2+ relatives and members of the poor and working classes from the Global South commit suicide at extremely high rates. What kind of suffering must our relatives be experiencing to decide that suicide is their only option?

In the United States, suicide is the second leading cause of death for people between the ages of 15–34, a reality that closely parallels statistics for the rest of the world, where suicide is the second leading cause of death for people aged 15–24. Studies vary wildly when it comes to determining whether suicides have increased or decreased under neoliberalism, but they agree that men commit suicide three to four times more often than women, although women typically attempt suicide three times more often than men and are twice as likely to experience depression.[9] LGBTQ2+ youth are three times more likely to attempt suicide than cisgender, heterosexual youth.[10] And 41 percent of transgender adults report having attempted suicide at some point in their lives.[11]

Although studies and statistics on suicide are incomplete, it is clear that suicide is linked to race, poverty, gender, and colonialism. For example, Arizona, New Mexico, Utah, Washington, Montana, South Dakota, and Wyoming rank among the states with the highest suicide rates in the country. What do these states have in common? They all have high Native populations. Native people die by suicide at rates higher than any other demographic in the United States, and our youth are especially at risk across the board—men, women, and gender nonconforming people alike. How often do we hear stories of youth

suicides—often in clusters of four or more within a short time period and geographic location—happening in Native communities? Youth suicide deaths are so common in Indian Country that it is impossible to talk about healthcare, mental health, gender, sexuality, education, housing, or incarceration without also talking about suicide. Our alarm—and our action—should match the magnitude of the crisis.

Native youth are the literal future of our nations—future caretakers and caretakers of the future. Every time a young Native person dies by suicide, we lose a relative who might have played an important role in leading our people into the future. Their deaths, whether by suicide or other forms of violence, are one of the most devastating realities we face as Indigenous revolutionaries engaged in the future-oriented project of decolonization. We simply cannot claim to be doing revolutionary work unless we are aggressively and proactively organizing to stop suicides among our youth, men, women, LGBTQ2+, and poor relatives.

There are particular areas that need our urgent attention. Access to mental health services in Indigenous communities is limited and often expensive. As a result, the correlation between mental health issues like depression and suicide rates are overlooked, especially for youth. Indigenous children face extremely high rates and types of violence from an early age. Violence accounts for 75 percent of deaths for Native youth between ages twelve and twenty.[12] There is a strong correlation between early exposure to violence, mental health, and suicide. More than 90 percent of people who died by suicide suffer from depression, have a substance abuse disorder, or both. We must address depression and substance abuse in order to address suicide.

However, this is not an issue that can be fixed through better services or suicide-prevention campaigns. Studies show that suicide rates are lower in Native communities that have strong self-determination over land, education, health, and governance. Of the thousands of

people who lived, worked, and struggled together during the occupation at Standing Rock in 2016, not a single one died by suicide. The resistance camps were dominated by Native people who are otherwise surrounded by the violence and death of colonialism that causes suicide in the first place. One would expect suicide to be as commonplace in the camps as any other Native community. But during that brief period of time, Indigenous people were free. Everyone was sheltered, fed, cared for, and welcomed into ceremonial spaces. Everyone had a special role in maintaining the camp and all community members had access to cultural knowledge and free education.

For many, it was the first time they received positive affirmation for being Indigenous, which resulted in pride and dignity. And it was not only Indigenous people who benefited from this Indigenous form of social and political organization. Non-Native community members in the camps were treated with the same dignity and respect as Native people. What we saw at Standing Rock was a truly self-governing, Indigenous-led form of self-determination. It was a liberated zone. We therefore know what works and what we need to do in order to reverse the trend of suicide for all people: restore dignity and Indigenous values. The only way this will happen is if everyone promotes decolonization, the return of Indigenous lands, and true self-determination for Indigenous people.

Area 7: Healthy, Sustainable, and Abundant Food

Food is not only considered physical sustenance, but also a connection to emotional and spiritual spaces that have nourished our people. As Winona LaDuke has argued, food security is necessary in order for a nation to have political independence. But because we exist in a capitalist system, food, like everything else, is subjected to

the logics of profit and class inequality. The result is that we are weak and dependent on processed foods, incapable of growing our own food and exerting true independence.

Despite the United States being the largest food exporter in the world and third in total food production, most poor and working-class people are forced to eat unhealthy food or simply go hungry. According to the United States Department of Agriculture (USDA), around forty-one million people in the United States face food insecurity, including thirteen million children.[13] What if the 30–40 percent of food produced in the United States that was wasted and dumped in landfills—over 161 billion pounds—was given to families in need?[14] Food insecurity is not only about lack of access to food; it is also about poor access to healthy and fresh foods for millions of people. "Food deserts" are an issue across the United States. From low-income communities of color to mostly white, conservative communities, food insecurity and lack of access are a significant problem.

Reservations are especially affected. Almost half of reservation residents have incomes three times lower than the federal poverty level. A household of five in 2019 had an annual income of less than $30,170. A 2014 report from the USDA found that fewer than 26 percent of reservation households live within one mile of a supermarket.[15] Moreover, of those living in extremely low-income conditions on reservations, less than 28 percent live within walking distance from a supermarket, whereas 64 percent of low-income individuals living in other parts of the United States can walk to get food.[16] This means half of all Native people living in reservations cannot afford the private vehicles or fuel required to make the long trips required to access grocery stores. Even if they do make it to a grocery store, they are barely able to afford even the cheapest food, which is filled with refined sugar, saturated fats, and carcinogens.

As if this were not enough, convenience stores located on reservations lack healthier food items. When available, the cost of a healthy diet is significantly higher. The solution for this problem cannot be found in creating more access to "affordable" foods by building more dollar stores or fast-food restaurants.

Across Indigenous communities, there is a new interest in food sovereignty. Although peasant communities in the Global South define food sovereigty as a right to control the food you grow and eat, Indigenous food sovereignty movements are focused on rekindling longstanding relationships with the land. Indigenous food sovereignty movements are about health revitalization, language conservation, and connecting youth with elders.[17]

We must build a food sovereignty movement to provide healthy, sustainable, and abundant food for everyone. You can promote food sovereignty by supporting local community food programs and co-ops, organizing a community garden and seed bank, financing and opening municipal-owned grocery stores, and creating community organizations that feed people. An excellent example of this is PotBangerz – Feed the Body Mission in St. Louis, Missouri. It was started to feed unsheltered people and adapted to feed thousands of protestors who participated in the Ferguson uprising in 2014 responding to the police murder of Michael Brown, and many others.

Area 8: Clean Water, Land, and Air

Decades of coal mining, uranium mining, and burning of coal in power plants that surround Indigenous lands have contributed to higher asthma rates and possibly contributes to greater instances of cancers in Indigenous communities. In the Permian Basin in Texas, an increase in fracking since the early 2000s has led to higher methane

rates that affect air quality. In the Pacific Northwest, the warming of waters and rising of sea levels due to climate change has affected land and water ecosystems and decimated salmon populations. And in the Midwest, Monsanto farms release chemicals into rivers that make water undrinkable and even dangerous to touch for millions. These acts of violence against Mother Earth have not gone unchallenged by Indigenous organizers.

In 2015, Diné farmers and ranchers in the Four Corners region of the United States organized to clean the Animas and San Juan Rivers after they were contaminated by the Gold King Mine spill. In early 2016, thousands of water protectors fought against the Dakota Access Pipeline to protect Mni Sose, or the Missouri River, which is one of the largest waterways in North America. In 2019, Indigenous people in Brazil, Paraguay, and Bolivia fought to stop the burning of their homelands in the Amazon, which many consider to be the result of deforestation. The twenty-first century has seen catastrophic assaults on the Earth and suppression of Indigenous caretakers who protect and defend the waters and lands that comprise the world's lungs and arteries. This devastation has happened in the name of profit. For the capitalists of the world, clean water and air do not matter so long as there is a buck to be made by plundering them. As a consequence, Earth—and all life that depends on her—is dying.

The environmental justice movement was started in the 1980s by poor Black communities seeking protection from the disastrous health effects of industrial pollution and toxic waste dumping, which disproportionately affect poor, Black, and Indigenous communities. However, nongovernmental (NGO) and nonprofit organizations dominate the environmental sector today. These organizations typically deploy a conservationist approach that uses law to protect nature from development. The problem with conservation is that

it seeks parity between these seemingly opposed goals as an ideal outcome. Conservationists often try to strike a compromise between protection and development to win their campaigns. The notion of "sustainability" is a formula that commonly drives this compromise. Sustainability describes a desired balance between industrial pollution and environmental health that allows everyone to win and feel good about protecting the environment.

However, even when they do win their campaigns—which are typically lawsuits and policy reforms—conservationists are only able to protect small amounts of land and water, which are typically already compromised by industry. This incremental and piecemeal approach to ensuring clean land, air, and water is depressing. It operates from a deficit rather than a position of strength. Conservation has certainly won some important gains for environmental justice, but it is ultimately a struggle for crumbs that offers defensive possibilities at best. Moreover, because of its emphasis on concession, it does not provide a strong foundation from which to build power, nor is it capable of advancing a strong analysis and stance on capitalism beyond asking ruling-class corporations to practice more sustainable or ethical forms of capitalism. Why would we continue to put energy and resources into an approach that has already admitted defeat in the face of capitalism?

We need a movement that decenters conservation and the NGOs and nonprofits that continue to consume considerable amounts of resources and power for conservation campaigns. These resources should be redistributed to the people and communities who hold the solutions and knowledge about how to fight for and take care of the land, water, and air: Indigenous people. Divesting from the nonprofit industrial complex is especially urgent given the reality we currently face on a planetary level: decolonization or extinction. We thus

encourage everyone to seriously question who we take leadership from in our movements. We recommend that all Indigenous people stop taking direction from NGOs and environmental nonprofits and begin to devise a new paradigm of struggle to address climate justice that does not reproduce the traps of conservation.

We should all be looking to grassroots Indigenous and frontline organizations in the Global South who are calling for far more visionary, militant, creative, and comprehensive climate justice programs than those that Global North environmentalists can offer. These movements tend to also have a strong ethical foundation when it comes to capitalism and US imperialism. We can contribute to and draw from these movements by educating and organizing to permanently halt fracking, mining, and all types of resource extraction in Indigenous communities. We can use the billions of dollars that are funneled into NGOs and nonprofits each year to create new jobs in land, air, and water restoration that will be lost by the demise of the extractive industry. We can unconditionally support Indigenous-led movements and grassroots organizations that protect air, land, and water. We can study and implement the People's Agreement of Cochabamba, Bolivia, which we reference throughout *The Red Deal*. And we can refuse to let capitalism destroy our future any longer.

Area 9: End Gender, Sexual, and Domestic Violence

Many of us are familiar with the epidemic of Missing and Murdered Indigenous Women, Girls, and Two-Spirit relatives (MMIWG2S), but what is often left out of the conversation are the conditions that many of these people experience prior to their deaths and disappearances. Rampant sexual violence and domestic abuse in Native households, both on- and off-reservation, create hostile environments

that render Native people more vulnerable to continued violence and death at the hands of multiple perpetrators, including the state, racist vigilantes, men, the extractivist industry, and non-Natives. The disturbing frequency of domestic and sexual violence among Native people is nothing other than a result of centuries of settler colonial violence and dispossession. Because Indigenous bodies stand in the way of access to the land and because women are seen as the producers of Native nations through the European heteropatriarchal lens, violence against women, particularly sexual violence, is used as means of separating Native people from the land. Nonmen represent alternative political orders that replicate Native nationhood. Violence upon queer and feminine bodies was used as a primary tactic for the obliteration of Indigenous governance structures.

For this reason, women and queer people, especially when in positions of power, are the biggest threat to settler projects of dispossession. Leanne Betasamosake Simpson states that sexual violence is an effective tool of conquest because of the overwhelming damage it inflicts upon families, lasting for generations and instilling shame and humiliation that discourages any efforts to resist. This use of sexual violence as a means of disconnecting Native people from their sources of strength—their families, cultures, traditions of resistance, and the land itself—persisted throughout the boarding school era where Native children were frequently subjected to sexual violence and physical abuse by teachers and school administrators, including Christian priests. After this era, Native women and families were stripped of their autonomy via forced sterilizations, lack of access to equitable prenatal and postnatal care, poor reproductive health services, poverty, assimilation, exotification, and objectification. Forced sterilizations are rumored to still take place in Indian Health Service facilities and misinformation about birth control, which is based

on racist assumptions about Indigenous women's promiscuity and dirtiness, is widespread.

This ongoing violence is not confined to just Native people. It deeply affects all colonized people worldwide. In consecutive reports released in 2017 and 2019, the United Nations revealed that women and girls die from domestic violence more than any other crime. This information was released in a global study on homicide that focused on gender-related killings. The study revealed that out of 87,000 women who were murdered around the world, 58 percent were killed by family members or partners, with 34 percent murdered by intimate partners, and 24 percent murdered by other family members.[18]

According to the Indian Law Resource Center, in the United States, violence against Indigenous women has reached unprecedented levels. Four out of five American Indian and Alaskan Native women have experienced violence, and one in two have experienced sexual violence.[19] Alaskan Native women continue to suffer the highest rate of forcible sexual assault and have reported rates of domestic violence up to ten times higher than the rest of the population. Native youth who see violence in the home—which are the majority—are 75 percent more likely to become a future victim or perpetrator of violence. As we note in Area 6, violence accounts for 75 percent of deaths for Native youth between the ages of twelve and twenty. More than 60 percent of Native youth have been recently exposed to violence in different sectors of their lives, including home, school, and other parts of their community.[20]

Native men also experience high rates of victimization. More than four in five American Indian and Alaskan Native men have experienced violence in their lifetime. Almost 28 percent have experienced sexual violence, over 43 percent have experienced physical violence by an intimate partner, and 73 percent have experienced

psychological aggression by an intimate partner.[21] Transgender relatives experience even higher rates of violence: 65 percent of American Indian and Alaskan Native respondents to the 2015 US transgender survey have been sexually assaulted at some point in their lifetimes. Nearly three-quarters (73 percent) of respondents experienced some form of intimate partner violence, including acts of coercive control. Nearly half (46 percent) of respondents who worked in the underground economy such as sex work and drug sales in the year prior to the survey's release were sexually assaulted during that year.[22]

Everyone deserves access to a safe, loving home and all of the resources required to heal from ongoing gender, sexual, and domestic violence. We must advocate for available resources for those fleeing domestic violence. We can build and support violence shelters that are mindful of the specific needs of Native women and easy to reach from rural reservation and urban spaces. Consider volunteering at already-existing shelters or organizing community members to provide safe spaces and basic necessities to those fleeing domestic violence. With the creation of mutual aid networks, people can organize call lists or online groups of those able to house or assist people fleeing domestic violence with basic necessities such as transportation, childcare, groceries, etc. We can promote access to accurate sexual education and the full range of reproductive health services by organizing campaigns that destigmatize sex, educate about safer sex practices, and advocate for body sovereignty and body positivity.

This includes the destigmatization of abortion, birth control, STI and HIV testing, and teaching youth about consent. Support the renewal of traditional, noncarceral birthing practices for women so they have control over their own reproductive health and the health of their children. Consider hosting teach-ins in your community

where important discussions about unlearning toxic masculinity and heteropatriarchal violence can be held. Provide spaces where individuals might be able to obtain more resources about sexual health, healthy relationships, mental health, and having these difficult conversations in the home.

Area 10: End Missing and Murdered Indigenous Women, Girls, and Two-Spirit Peoples

The genocide of MMIWG2S is rarely framed as an example of "bordertown violence," which is itself often described as a recent phenomenon. Bordertown violence is a form of state violence that has upheld the colonial project of resource exploitation, relocation, displacement and genocide since the first military outposts and forts were constructed along the Western "frontier" of the fledgling United States. Bordertown violence is nothing more than contemporary frontier violence. Most bordertowns today were once centers of the most horrendous frontier violence. Places like Chamberlain, South Dakota and Gallup, New Mexico served as centers of trade where white settlers not only sold and traded goods like fur, but lured, sold, and kidnapped Native women and girls to be sex trafficked to soldiers and traders who manned these outposts and forts. Bordertowns are the original man camps. One of the first lines of struggle to end MMIWG2S is to end bordertown violence and vice versa.

Today most people are familiar with man camps as a result of gas and oil extractivist projects. The presence of gas and oil makes it clear that the United States never stopped its project of displacement and elimination of Native people. The land continues to be stolen for these projects. The poorest and most vulnerable communities

are coerced into selling their land to multinational oil companies yet remain in poverty once corporations have taken all the land can offer. Meanwhile, the richest in the world continue to siphon wealth from these communities. As a result of this continual displacement, 71 percent of Indigenous people live in urban spaces.

There is no escape from this cycle of violence on or off the reservation. MMIWG2S is a continuous and pervasive form of violence that affects every corner of our communities. Homicide is the third leading cause of death for Native women in the United States, regardless of where they live. In a recent report from the Urban Indian Health Institute (UIHI), the city of Albuquerque, which has one of the largest urban Native populations in the country, was found to have high rates of MMIWG2S.[23] This is no coincidence, as Albuquerque is a bordertown in a state that depends on gas and oil development to fund important social services.

New Mexico is essentially one large man camp, which also helps to explain why it has the highest number of MMIWG2S cases compared to any other state. Despite these numbers, the Santa Fe Police Department admitted to not keeping track of MMIWG2S and domestic violence cases because "most Native women have Spanish surnames." This means that a state already at the top of the charts when it comes to MMIWG2S likely has more cases, yet police do almost nothing to solve these cases or even track them. The Albuquerque Police Department (APD), for example, was notorious for refusing to test sexual assault evidence kits and had a backlog of more than 5,500 that sat in city custody for years until grassroots pressure, followed by a Department of Justice investigation, forced the city to put resources towards processing the kits in 2018. How many MMIWG2S cases might have been solved—or prevented—had the APD simply tested these kits in a timely and competent manner?

Countless efforts to bring awareness through federal legislation and state task forces are created while the ongoing settler violence continues. Prominent politicians and advocates in the state—including many Native women—continue to propose an increase in policing as the primary solution for ending the crisis. Calls for better policing have been accompanied by national attention to MMIWG2S, which in 2020 resulted in the Trump administration creating a special task force called "Operation Lady Justice" to investigate "the scope and nature of the issues regarding missing and murdered American Indians and Alaska Natives."

The phrase "MMIWG2S" now appears on everything from campaign slogans to t-shirts to stickers to water bottles. It is a prominent hashtag on social media. And with the election of Native women like Deb Haaland—who is originally from Laguna Pueblo in New Mexico and now represents a district in Albuquerque with high numbers of MMIWG2S—to US Congress in 2018, 2019 was officially declared "The Year of the Native Woman." While we are encouraged by this attention to MMIWG2S, we remind our readers that the movement to stop gender and sexual violence against Native relatives began with radical grassroots organizations formed by everyday Native women. Unlike these politicians and nonprofits, grassroots organizations have never separated their calls for justice from larger issues like resource extraction, land return, and sovereignty. Women of All Red Nations, Idle No More, and now, The Red Nation, will continue to advocate for an end to MMIWG2S by demanding nothing less than full decolonization.

It is clear that we cannot depend on state institutions to put an end to MMIWG2S; this includes cops. We cannot depend on cops to take MMIWG2S cases seriously when over 40 percent are domestic abusers themselves and perpetrate much of the violence that Native

people experience more generally.[24] Though Native people make up less than 1 percent of the US population, they are murdered by police at the highest rates. Cops are part of the problem, NOT the solution. We must also be honest about the fact that our LGBTQ2+ relatives experience domestic violence and police violence in bordertowns at the highest rates. Because they are frequently disowned by families and discriminated against in workplaces, they can become dependent on underground economies like sex work, which makes them more susceptible to trafficking that takes place in and around man camps, as well as police violence because of criminalization.

As we note in the previous section, domestic violence is normalized and often underreported because it occurs so often in Native homes, families, and intimate relationships. It is so common that it is often not understood as a form of violence! We need to change how we think about violence; violence is not just about war or extreme physical altercations. The most common form of violence is domestic violence and the source of the violence is heteropatriarchy.

What can we do about this crisis? Host actions, demonstrations, or protests when there is no justice for MMIWG2S. Organizations already doing vital work are Sovereign Bodies Institute, the Coalition to Stop Violence Against Native Women, and Native Youth Sexual Health Network. Start your own campaign if there is nothing being organized around you. Host workshops, study groups, fundraisers, or other events that bring awareness to MMIWG2S.

When Diné mother Loreal Tsingine was murdered by racist cop Austin Shipley in the bordertown of Winslow, Arizona in 2016, he was left free to roam the streets. The Red Nation, along with Loreal's family, demanded action and held a number of protests, which led to the creation of the Border Town Justice Coalition, a report on bordertown violence, and an investigation by the Navajo Nation of the Winslow

Police Department. Create accessible literature and online documents that can be easily circulated within your community that contain facts about MMIWG2S and have a larger analysis of its connections to hetero-patriarchy, resource extraction, and colonialism. It is important to have conversations with family about how negative attitudes about women and LGBTQ2+ relatives, as well as our dependency on fossil fuel revenues and normalization of male privilege, contributes to this epidemic.

HEAL OUR PLANET

Reinvest in Our Common Future

Introduction

There is no hope for restoring the planet's fragile and dying eco-systems without Indigenous liberation. This is not an exaggeration. It's the simple truth. Indigenous people understand the choice that confronts us: decolonization or extinction. We have unequivocally renewed our bonds with the Earth, implementing intellectual traditions in the movements for decolonization. There is no turning back; these bonds are sacred and will never be broken. This is why Indigenous water protectors and land defenders throughout the world are criminalized and assassinated on a daily basis. We have chosen life and therefore we have been marked for death.

Despite this grim reality, Indigenous people continue to caretake the land, even under threat of daily attack. The labor that Indigenous water protectors, land defenders, and treaty defenders perform is crucial to our species. We depend upon caretakers for both social and biological reproduction. Humanity would not exist without caretakers. But caretaking is labor. It takes work to plant crops. It takes work to hunt. It takes work to raise children. It takes work to clean homes. It takes work to break down a buffalo. It takes work to learn the properties of traditional medicines.

Healing the planet is ultimately about creating infrastructures of caretaking that will replace infrastructures of capitalism. Capitalism is contrary to life. Caretaking promotes life. As we note throughout this book, caretaking is at the center of contemporary Indigenous movements for decolonization and liberation. We therefore look to these movements for guidance on building infrastructures of caretaking that have the potential to produce caretaking economies and caretaking jobs now and in the future. We also look to the infrastructure of caretaking that is currently

emerging where capitalist nation-states have failed to save lives from COVID-19.

Under the current system of global capitalism, caretaking is undervalued and often unrecognized as a form of labor. Caretakers like parents, land defenders, and water protectors make up a huge percentage of workers who produce the social and material means by which we live, yet they are not paid. In a world being reshaped by a pandemic, caretakers have become the most important sector of workers, not only by saving people's lives but also keeping whole families and communities afloat. Mutual aid networks populated by caretakers are proliferating, providing relief to the most vulnerable, and paving the way for robust caretaking economies to replace the crumbling system of global capitalism. Current mutual aid networks are neither state-sanctioned nor state-funded efforts; they are entirely people-led and the result of working-class solidarity between nurses, service providers, students, domestic workers, migrant farmers, and families. Mutual aid networks affirm life by caretaking for humanity rather than denying life by abandoning and exploiting humanity. The monumental challenge we face is how to turn caretaking labor into life-affirming mass movements that can topple global capitalism once the emergency conditions of the pandemic lift.

Only when we are able to mount a real threat to the hegemony of global capitalism through such movements will we be able to heal the planet. Like the development of mass movements, affirming our relationship with the land is not optional if we wish to avoid extinction. This is not some mystical vision where we go out and hug trees, it is a serious agenda for decolonization that requires comprehensive land-return programs and funding for mass, Indigenous-led land-restoration projects. Healthy reciprocity with the environment also depends upon Indigenous people having unrestricted access

to land, unencumbered by colonial borders and free of harassment from agents of the state.

We understand the land is our means of production as Indigenous people; this is why decolonization and land return are not metaphors. Land is also the means of production for settler economies, which require property as a basic building block (often called "primitive accumulation" by Marxists) for amassing capital and power. We cannot successfully wage class war until Indigenous land repatriation is taken seriously as a precursor to seizing the means of production more broadly. US imperialism—the greatest threat to the future of the planet—will never end if land remains in the hands of settler capitalists. The collective future of us all depends upon the ability of Indigenous caretakers to work with the land, restore its health, and reestablish balance in our relations.

With threats like radioactive contamination, wildfires, chemical pollution, and biodiversity loss, we will also need to seek new and alternative technologies. This is something Indigenous people embrace because we have always been technological innovators, scientists, and engineers. But as we know, capitalists have a monopoly on technology, with the majority of the most advanced technologies being used for war efforts. Scientists are denied funding for projects that are not considered profitable or that directly disrupt the flow of capital to the already wealthy. What if technology was created for the benefit of all life on Earth? In order to answer this question, we must turn to Indigenous knowledge. The following pages prove that our traditions of science, technology, and diplomacy are key to ensuring a future for all living beings on this planet.

Trauma-informed thinking has taken over Indigenous governments, institutions, nonprofits, revenue streams, and even movements. Like electoral politics, trauma-based healing sucks all the

political and emotional energy out of the room, leaving little space for other possibilities and visions for change. The narrowing of our collective energies into trauma has come at the expense of building vibrant and militant struggles for liberation with other colonized and oppressed peoples of the world. Rather than allying with revolutionary movements in the Global South to overturn US imperialism once and for all, we argue on social media and academic panels about injury: who is more injured and who injures more. This is entirely a First World discourse. Movements outside the United States rarely traffic in the language of trauma and injury to develop political positions or tactics of organizing.

What does it mean to take up healing as a revolutionary concept, one that transcends the neoliberal realm of individual trauma and allows us to imagine a world that prioritizes collective well-being and healthy relationships? In this time of a global pandemic, we must reclaim healing from the neoliberal individualism afforded to trauma and injury and instead globalize our efforts. The Red Deal advocates for healing our bodies and the planet, but not from individual trauma alone. We must heal from colonialism and capitalism—together. "You have to quit crying on the shoulder of the man who stole your land," the late Secwépmc elder Arthur Manuel was fond of saying.[1] The saying has an acute resonance in Canada, where the Truth and Reconciliation Commission listened to millions of hours of Indigenous testimony documenting the abuses at the hands of residential schools and the intergenerational trauma that ensued. While the testimony was cathartic and documented actual instances of genocide, not a single scrap of Indigenous land was returned and colonialism didn't end.

The cunning politics of injury has come to define our era, where state and corporate perpetrators of violence and genocide are asked

to—or position themselves—as purveyors of "justice" while entirely sidestepping the question of colonialism and imperialism. Prior to this era of so-called reconciliation, liberation was on the horizon of struggle. Today, the horizon has become our further incorporation into the settler state and US imperialism.

Instead of finding a seat at the table, we ask that this table get off our lands. We are more defined by our dreams of liberation and freedom and we refuse to be defined by trauma and violence narratives, as hapless subjects rather than active agents of history. Liberation and freedom, no less and no more, defines healing for us. COVID-19 is a harsh but crucial lesson about the need for collective healing, which will require militant movements to liberate the planet from systems and structures that target whole nations and species. Although there are many points of entry into this global struggle, there can be no doubt that Indigenous movements for decolonization and liberation must be at the center of our collective efforts.

Area 1: Clean Sustainable Energy

The world is transitioning from fossil fuels to clean and renewable energies, but not fast enough. Resource extraction is still ravaging Indigenous, Black, migrant, and other-than-human communities. The Amazon forest fire of 2019 resulted in the burning of over 2 million acres and the assassination of Guajajara Indigenous leader and land defender, Paulo Paulino, all in the name of mining and logging. In early 2020, Canada invaded sovereign Wet'suwet'en territory to remove Unist'ot'en land defenders who had successfully stopped construction of the Coastal GasLink pipeline for close to a decade. Infrastructure projects like the pipeline that carries natural gas from fracking fields

to ports for international export violate Wet'suwet'en sovereignty. The Navajo Nation is still one of largest resource colonies in the United States, supplying energy through coal and natural gas conversion to some of the largest cities in the American West while many of its own citizens live without basic infrastructure like clean water and electricity. For Indigenous and poor communities throughout Turtle Island, the fracking revolution of the past decade has been particularly violent. Fracking is a type of drilling that injects chemicals and water into the ground to break up underlying shale rock, releasing the oil and natural gas contained within it.

Fracking produces more natural gas than crude oil for the US economy; two-thirds of natural gas in the United States comes from fracking, while approximately 50 percent of the nation's crude oil is procured through the same method. Corporations like TC Energy—formerly TransCanada, the corporation that built the Dakota Access Pipeline—claim that natural gas is one of the world's cleanest and safest energy sources. Natural gas is often called "clean" because it emits 50 percent less carbon than coal when you burn it. Governments like the state of New Mexico have partnered with fracking corporations to create shiny public relations campaigns about the benefits of natural gas as a bridge fuel that will help the planet transition from dirty fuel sources like coal into zero-net carbon renewable sources. Native people know the truth about this so-called clean energy. While the natural gas boom has created billions in profits for extractive corporations, governments, and investors, the fracking required to extract natural gas from below the Earth's surface has devastated Indigenous communities in the eastern region of Navajo Nation.

Meanwhile, extractive corporations are investing billions in renewable energy technologies to ensure they have a new source of

profit once "dirty" energy is phased out in favor of "clean" sources. Renewable energy corporations and start-ups proliferate, creating a new class of millionaires and billionaires who invest in green technology to profit while proclaiming they are saving the planet. The United States backs right-wing coups in Indigenous nations like Bolivia to access green energy sources like lithium. Whether extractive capitalism or green capitalism, profit is all the ruling class cares about: not the future of humanity; not Indigenous sovereignty; not the health of the Earth. It is therefore crucial that we imagine and organize for new sustainable energy initiatives led by Indigenous people.

Indigenous people have lived sustainably since time immemorial and can continue to live in reciprocity with all those we share the Earth with. Sustainable does not mean primitive. We must reclaim Indigenous intellectual traditions of the Western Hemisphere, which have some of the most advanced technology in human history. We have millennia-old mathematical and scientific theories allowing us to track the movement of the solar system, map out stars and galaxies, and create functional plumbing and aqueduct systems. We had these technologies long before Europeans discovered such things. Science and technology have never been at odds with Indigenous lifeways; it is only because of capitalism's monopoly on technology that science is used to destroy the planet. Science and technology should serve the needs of the people rather than profit or war. Capitalism is incapable of equitably distributing the technology and value that is created, even when it is towards green capitalism. Green energy jobs are often touted as the rationale for promoting renewable energy projects. However, if we look at renewable energy projects like Kayenta Solar Project, Moapa Southern Paiute Solar Project, and the Tsilhqot'in Solar Farm, the majority of employment for tribal members is temporary and only comes from construction and planning.

The maintenance is done by outside contractors. From vision to completion, solar jobs are not a sustainable source of jobs for local communities unless maintenance, monitoring, and remediation are taken into account. Saying that renewable energy will "create more jobs" simply isn't enough. We must have a clear understanding of the spectrum of labor that goes into green energy and demand that local communities—not private contractors—work these jobs. The materials used in solar panel systems are extremely important to consider. Lithium-ion batteries, according to the US Department of Energy, are and will be the main storage of renewable energies.

Lithium-ion batteries are made from two main minerals: cobalt and lithium. The Democratic Republic of Congo holds 60 percent of the world's cobalt, while Bolivia holds 70 percent of the world's lithium.[2] Both countries face heavy exploitation by the world's economic powers like the US, China, Canada, France, and India. While these countries are supplying the Global North with green energy for the future, they remain some of the poorest nations in the world. We must not replicate the injustices and inequalities between the Global North and Global South that exist under our current structure of global capitalism by simply replacing fossil fuel extraction with renewable energy extraction. Even with the transition to green energy, the capitalist (and colonial) relation remains intact. This is called imperialism, whereby the wealth and power of Global North nations depends entirely upon the poverty and exploitation of Global South nations. We must fight against a system that deems the world's poor and Indigenous expendable for the sake of progress and profit.

We must ensure that all corporate polluters be held accountable and pay for full remediation of the land and reparations to the people who have felt the impacts of extraction for generations. This can be accomplished with boycotts and divestment campaigns or by urging

tribal leaders to break contracts with corporate polluters. Regardless of how clean and green the technology is, the process by which corporations extract value from Indigenous life for the benefit of settler colonialism remains the same. We will educate tribal communities on the histories of resource extraction. And, we will organize to stop all forms of energy extraction from Native communities and lands, whether it is coal mining, fracking, or solar farms.

Now more than ever we need people to understand that we have to actively create the world we want to live in. Man-made disasters like climate change and the unnecessary spread of COVID-19 are not manifestations of "the Earth healing itself." Such deadly events are a direct result of the actions of those who pillage the Earth: the ruling class. These capitalists view the Earth as a resource to be exploited instead of a relative to be protected. Wherever you are, create campaigns that pinpoint the central role of capitalism in creating this suffering, and the need to dismantle capitalism for the sake of our common future.

Area 2: Traditional and Sustainable Agriculture

Indigenous people have always been farmers and caretakers of land. Worldwide, more than half of the crops grown today originated in what is now called the Americas. Every potato in Ireland, tomato in Italy, and chili in Thailand was cultivated here first. We adjusted our lifeways to maintain sustainability. For example, when Pueblo peoples migrated from certain areas, it was due to the realization that irrigation farming alone was unsustainable in times of severe drought. This led to the development of dry farming methods. Simultaneously, areas where natural food systems already existed were nurtured. Forest management was crucial in

maintaining healthy watersheds, minimizing fire damage, and promoting healthy game animals and grasslands.

For generations, Indigenous people in what is now called California developed ways of modifying nature to not only benefit themselves but the entire ecosystem. Some of these modifications included the pruning of trees to encourage fruit and nut production, the burning of meadowlands to create pastures that could support animal life, and selective harvesting of plants to encourage plant production.[3] For years, scientific racism has worked to invalidate and exclude land-based knowledge and wisdom, such as the fire suppression regimes imposed by Spanish and American settlers who prohibited California tribes from practicing the controlled burns they had used to maintain the West Coast's forests. Modern science is only now recognizing the benefits of Indigenous knowledge, turning in particular to controlled burns to prevent devastating and severe wildfires in the Western states, while at the same time refusing to restore lands to Indigenous experts. The efforts by many tribes to acquire lands stolen from them in order to properly caretake and restore them should be supported widely, as Indigenous people are critical to sustainable ecosystems.

Extractivism and militarization on Native lands disrupted our land-based economies, which had always allowed for sustainable food production. One of the first weapons of colonial violence was to destroy crops and food systems in order to weaken people, often coinciding with the forced adoption of non-Native diets and outlawing the cultivation of traditional foods. For example, Spanish settlers outlawed the Mayan and Aztec peoples from growing amaranth, even going so far as to cut off the hands of anyone caught growing it. Later, in Pueblo communities, a tithe of the best of a family's crops had to be turned over to the Spanish missionaries at the end of each season

or they would face harsh punishment. Families were required to fill up the length of a manta (traditional wraparound dress) with food that was then seized. Imperial borders have inhibited the flow of the seed trade and knowledge-sharing practices amongst Native people throughout Turtle Island.

Historically, Native communities would have preserved seeds by sharing them with other communities so that certain plants wouldn't go extinct. They also actively worked to strengthen crop diversity. The forced relocation and displacement of Native nations separated us from our lands, medicines, spiritual sites, and food sources. Indigenous people experience some of the highest rates of food insecurity. It is unrealistic to expect the most marginalized to make a full return to land-based agriculture as a primary means of sustenance. We know the crushing weight of capitalism and land theft has forced us into the wage economy. Oftentimes, the jobs available force a separation of people from their lands. We know that we cannot heal lands and the subsistence they provide until capitalism and colonialism no longer exist. The blatant theft of Native lands—for resource extraction, settlement, big agriculture, military projects, etc.—is directly to blame for this epidemic of food scarcity. Projects of extraction and militarization prevent people from living off the land, and long after they are gone, they leave the land poisoned. Radioactive contamination of our lands leaves them unusable for centuries.

The term "food sovereignty" was first defined in 1996 by La Via Campesina, an international group of peasants and small-scale farmers who sought to articulate a common response to neoliberalism and the dominant market economy, and to defend their rights to land and seeds.[4] Food sovereignty has since been taken up by many Indigenous people worldwide. Seed sovereignty is the right of producers to breed, harvest, and exchange diverse and traditional

Indigenous seeds outside patents and the market economy and can be understood within the broader framework of food sovereignty. Seeds also have very specific ties to the birthwork movement, with the seed being understood as a womb and representing a life source. For some Native people, seeds themselves are even required in ceremonies following the birth of a child.

Seed sovereignty is constantly threatened by commodity culture through big agricultural seed patents, cross-pollination with genetically engineered contaminates, and laws catering to agricultural companies that make traditional seeds illegal to grow and possess. The genetic mutation of seeds through cross-pollination from GMOs, for example, can have a deleterious effect on the offspring of the plant. And likewise, the experiences and environmental exposures, whether negative or positive, can impact three generations in one pregnancy. A human fetus develops every egg they will ever have while still in utero in the womb. If a biological parent is exposed to contaminants, their unfertilized eggs are also exposed. Seeds have cultural connotations related to birth, belonging to a place, and ceremonies around how we claim our kin. Food is quite literally medicine and a cultural foundation for a community to thrive.

Imperial borders directly affect our trade and seed sharing with our relatives internationally that we have traditionally traded with, while big agriculture actively suppresses and kills the varieties of sacred foods and plants in favor of mass-produced GMOs. Food monopoly tycoons are trying to patent Indigenous seeds we have grown since time immemorial, therefore stealing and monopolizing sacred life-sustaining plants. The introduction of big agricultural crops into small Indigenous economies across Turtle Island is systematically destroying local economies, as they cannot compete with price differentials. In Mexico, the birthplace of corn, GMO seed companies

drastically reduced the price of corn so much that local markets crashed, sparking a movement calling for the banning of GMO seeds across regions.

Indigenous people, on and off the reservation, need foods that are whole, healthy, and Indigenous in their diet. Children, elders, and birth-givers are the most marginalized groups for food security. While Native land is stolen for big agricultural projects, Native people are not allowed to access the goods grown on their own lands. The market sees that these goods are exported elsewhere making it impossible for local subsistence economies to exist, meanwhile the state neglects Native communities that lack infrastructure such as grocery stores to ensure nutritious foods are accessible. Capitalism is why only the cheapest foods are able to make it to the most rural areas. Even in the event that healthy food is available it is often unaffordable. It is easier and more convenient for someone struggling to survive and working full-time to buy ready-made foods than it is to access foods that are locally grown and contain less chemicals and a smaller carbon footprint, since the distance between farm and table is shorter. It is cheaper and therefore more profitable to sell unhealthy foods that can sit on a shelf or be prepared in a matter of minutes, but less healthy for the consumer. The priority is profit in this system. It is also the reason why healthy foods are inaccessible for low-income families. In rural and urban communities this translates into having to travel great distances (and therefore spend more income) to get to a grocery store that sells healthy food at affordable prices.

Big agricultural projects should be understood as projects of resource extraction. Resource extraction depletes and pollutes the soil, making the land unusable for generations and minimizing available land for growing food. This creates the need for expensive,

long-term environmental restoration. Rather than caretake the land and see that it is restored for long-term food production, federal food programs—such as commodity distribution programs—try to compensate for the destruction capitalism and colonialism have caused to Native food systems. However, distributing foods that are not Indigenous has a negative impact on health and well-being in the long-term, creating issues like obesity, diabetes, cardiovascular disease, and other negative health impacts.[5]

Land Return

Our land, air, and waterways are polluted from capitalist endeavors, government mismanagement, and militarization. Traditional caregiving and sustainability do not disrespect or cut kinship with our land, water, air, and other-than-human relatives. Our mountain relatives are under military control and have been contaminated with nuclear waste and radiation; from contaminated water to contaminated animals and plants, and even the clay we use. This has affected every corner of life and our ability to sustain our relatives. This catastrophic offense will take years beyond our generation's lifetimes to clean and restore.

Having control over our ancestral territories is vital to our ability to care for them and is a generations-long pathway to true sustainability. Only when land is restored and returned can we begin to rebuild our economies and our nations with true sovereignty. Having a say in how the land is cared for would allow us reassert our relations with the land and our nonhuman relatives, which is the basis upon which Indigenous people define their nations and sovereignty.

Remediation

In places where Native ancestral homelands have been heavily polluted or diminished by resource extraction or militarization, the use of contemporary agricultural and horticultural practices may need to be taken up alongside traditional knowledge. We can incorporate hydroponic and aquaponic food systems into our lifeways while the land is in remediation from extractive and military projects that have caused immense devastation. Hydroponics and aquaponics allow food to be grown without being planted in the soil, or using ground water, and allow food to be grown indoors throughout the year. For Indigenous people, we can decolonize and restore balance and harmony to our food security and sovereignty through planting community gardens using our planting, harvesting, and ditch-work songs. We can use our knowledge of waterways, seed storage, seed exchange, dry farming, and waffle gardens to revive our gardening traditions. We can do this in a way that is culturally and spiritually grounded, so our prayers support the health and well-being of our communities.

Everyone can help to restore Indigenous seed economies by trading with Indigenous folks around the world. Historically we have had elaborate trade networks in place which allowed for the transfer and trade of seeds, meats, and agricultural knowledge. Oral histories of Pueblo people tell of the way we would create seed repositories in other communities, sometimes hundreds of miles away, to protect these crops from the devastation of European invasion where food sources were often targeted for destruction. We can disregard imperial borders imposed on us by reinvigorating these noncapitalist, ancestral trade networks. We can revive and re-integrate traditional ways of harvest management through cooperation and exchange with others, thereby strengthening traditional and sustainable economies.

In order to survive current challenges—and any future challenges—to our food sources, we suggest remaining flexible, open, and willing to learn new ways to be healthy. This includes how food is prepared and handled. Having direct contact from seed planting to harvest honors traditional food sovereignty. We suggest reviving old recipes and creating new recipes in which nutrient-rich foods are centered, where fruits and vegetables are our main source of vitamins. The widespread labeling of foods containing genetically engineered and transgenic ingredients must be mandated for food justice, allowing people the option of informed consent for what they are consuming. We must be in solidarity with Indigenous communities globally, in shared resistance to banning GMO and transgenic seeds, and work towards creating "genetically engineered free zones" across nations. We look to the work already being done by the New Mexico Food and Seed Sovereignty Alliance to preserve traditional and sustainable agriculture and, the Traditional Native American Farmers Association (TNAFA) and the New Mexico Acequia Association (NMAA) collaboration on "A Declaration of Seed Sovereignty: A Living Document for New Mexico," which offers thirty points highlighting the devastation of Indigenous land and agriculture and lays out a framework for their restoration.[6]

We know that as a result of being forced into the capitalist economy, Native nations have been pressured into selling their land and resources, making contracts with extractivist corporations in the name of "economic development." Native nations are only allowed to engage in economic development in just a few ways as domestic dependent nations; gaming, tourism, and the selling of land and resources are among the most common. For this reason, many tribal governments actively work with extractvist corporations or military branches for the minuscule profit that can be gained from allowing such occupation.

We can pressure our tribal governments to cut ties with corporate polluters who aid the devastation of land in the name of economic development. We can divest from big banks that fund extractive projects both as individuals and as Native nations. We can stand against continued land devastation by organizing and participating in protests, blockades, and encampments. We can urge our tribal governments to assert their sovereignty and rebuild our relationships with Native peoples beyond US borders, to restore knowledge and trade. This is how we can heal the land and rebuild our own economic frameworks to end dependence on the settler state.

Area 3: Land, Water, Air, and Animal Restoration

Recent studies show that although the world's 370 million Indigenous people make up less than 5 percent of the total human population, traditional Indigenous territories encompass between 22–25 percent of the world's land surface and coincide with areas that hold 80–90 percent of the planet's biodiversity. The greatest diversity of Indigenous groups exist within the tropical forests of the Americas, Africa, and Asia, and 11 percent of the world's forests are legally "owned" by Indigenous peoples and communities. These forests—like the Amazon—are the lungs of the world, producing about 20 percent of the oxygen in our Earth's atmosphere. Climate research indicates that one of the most alarming aspects of the current environmental crisis is the loss of biodiversity, which affects human survival by interfering with crucial ecosystem maintenance such as pollination and water purification. Loss of biodiversity threatens the land, air, and water; relatives with whom we share this world.

Of the four billion species that have evolved over the last three-and-a-half billion years, 99 percent have gone extinct. That rate

of extinction had always been balanced by the evolution of new species. But there have been five exceptions to this pattern; five instances of mass extinction when the rate of species loss was so great that the biodiversity of the Earth was drastically reduced. These instances were caused by sudden cataclysmic events such as a series of massive volcanic outbursts, major asteroid impacts, or dramatic sea level change.

A recent study shows that there has been an increasingly rapid rate of species loss over the last few centuries when compared to the "normal" rate of extinctions. These findings show species are going extinct at a rate of up to 100 times the background rate. In other words: extinction rates have reached levels unparalleled since the dinosaurs died out sixty-six million years ago. There is no longer any doubt that we have entered the sixth mass extinction in Earth's history. After the last mass extinction event that caused the extinction of the dinosaurs, it took hundreds of thousands of years for species biodiversity to recover. Extinctions and reductions in biodiversity are directly linked to land degradation: in places where the health of the land has been destroyed through pollution and hyper-exploitation, biodiversity diminishes. Yet, where Indigenous people have freedom to caretake the land, biodiversity flourishes. This is because, as opposed to capitalism, Indigenous people around the world do not see themselves as separate from the land.

For us, land, plants, animals, and water are our relatives. The soil is alive and interacting with the air, waterways, and all other-than-human creatures. The Indigenous perspective looks forward to the future of our children, our children's children, and to the well-being of all living things. It also looks back to the wisdom of our ancestors. This intimate relationship between past, present, and future allows for close observation of the interactions and interdependencies

between species across time and space. It allows for reverence of the land in which humans live in balance with all other beings.

Water, air, animal, and human restoration depends upon the health of the land. Restoring the land, and our commitment to living in balance with our relatives, is thus key to securing a future for all. Current statistics about mass extinction, biodiversity, and air quality show irrefutably that land cannot simply be "restored" by technological fixes or environmental protections adjudicated in settler institutions. Land restoration must center Indigenous land stewardship and multi-species caretaking—and thus the mass return of land to Indigenous nations and the implementation of true Indigenous self-determination—if we are to have any hope of a future on this planet.

Recommendations

Indigenous people have played a key role in climate change mitigation and adaptation. In New Zealand, for example, Māori people have advocated for the rights of the sacred Whanganui River which has been given the status of personhood for its protection.[7] We can promote the return of land to Indigenous people wherever we are. Popular tactics for Indigenous land return include land trust campaigns and honor taxes, whereby trusts are created with the purpose of purchasing land back, or where Native nations occupied by cities assert that occupiers pay the tribe an "honor tax." It is easy to see that Indigenous people are the most suited and knowledgeable caretakers of the land. Giving land back to Indigenous people is the first step in land restoration.

Capitalism, in its unrelenting demand for profit, uses and destroys the land with no consideration for future generations. We

must understand that capitalism is the enemy of the future. It does not see the land as a living thing to be cared for and respected, but simply another tool with which to satisfy greed.

Extractive industries, logging, encroaching infrastructure, deforestation, and improper agricultural practices such as monocropping and overgrazing, all contribute to a decline in soil structure. Soil degradation, in the form of salt and water imbalances, is often caused by waste disposal, chemical pollutants, and leaking pipelines. The compression of soil, which decreases air and water retention, is the result of soil being too compacted by heavy machinery, floods, and building structures. Excessive irrigation and fertilizers induce soil fertility depletion, while logging and deforestation lead to accelerated erosion. Healthy soil is essential for the production of vegetation. A diversity of vegetation attracts insects, birds, and other animals that serve important functions in the maintenance of ecosystems. Land restoration is imperative to restoring biodiversity. Biodiversity is the key to a vibrant and thriving planet.

We must design ecological restoration projects across the globe. Traditional practices for ecological restoration include revegetation by combining native, domestic, and wild plant species, crop rotation, agroforestry, burning practices (e.g., as utilized by the Aboriginal people of Australia), intercropping, and water harvesting. These practices are designed to increase the health of the soil, protect crops, and create biodiversity.

Anyone can promote food sovereignty in their local context by gardening, on a small or large scale. Stewardship of the land ensures food security, which is increasingly important in these times of COVID-19. Find, join, and help a local organization that is pushing back against pollution or contamination caused by industry and resource extraction.

Ending all forms of toxic capitalism will take us a long way in restoring the land to health. The two greatest threats faced by Indigenous peoples are the loss of land and the loss of ancestral knowledge. This is as serious a threat as the massive extinction of species on Earth. Ancestral wisdom and Traditional Ecological Knowledge (TEK) must be preserved and protected. Gatherings of elders where they share their knowledge with tribal members and other Indigenous groups can be an effective mechanism for ensuring that knowledge is not lost, especially if Indigenous youth are active participants. Support for Indigenous women's networks is also needed, as they are the carriers of ancestral knowledge.

Area 4: Protection and Restoration of Sacred Sites

The United States is an empire bringing death and destruction to those within its grasp. Those who try to protect the land from imperial violence are cast as obstacles, and deemed expendable and criminal. In 2016, we saw the brutalization of water protectors at Standing Rock by militarized police. Oil and gas industries continue to target Chaco Canyon and mark the surrounding communities as sacrifice zones. In 2019, thirty-three elders were arrested for blocking access to to Mauna Kea for construction of the Thirty Meter Telescope. Tohono O'odham relatives face daily harassment and restriction of movement in their own homelands by US Border Patrol agents. Police officers demand consent (how can you 'demand' consent?) at gunpoint, yet it is the Wet'suwet'en who are criminalized for protecting their territory. Indigenous land defenders of the Amazon are murdered for protecting forests that sustain life for the entire planet.

The criminalization of land defenders and water protectors is a tactic to eliminate and uproot Indigenous peoples and other-than-human

relatives. Indigenous peoples will always resist imperialism and capitalist development because we recognize the United States as an invader. We understand that protecting our relatives—land, water, air, ancestors, women, two-spirit, animals, medicines, children, and others—is at the heart of our customary forms of governance. It is what makes us who we are. While phrases that emphasize the sacred, including "sacred sites," "women are sacred," and "we are sacred" are now common for describing why we should practice the art of protection, at its base, protecting is simply about being a good relative. Given the violence and destruction that US imperialism forces upon us, protecting our relatives is a direct rejection of capitalism and empire. We demand the liberation of all our relatives. We demand a future.

The Red Deal extends solidarity to Indigenous peoples around the world who are fighting to protect our relatives from the ongoing ravages of imperialism. The *United Nations Declaration on the Rights of Indigenous Peoples* (UNDRIP) explicitly states in Article 25, "Indigenous peoples have the right to maintain and strengthen their distinctive spiritual relationship with their traditionally owned or otherwise occupied and used lands, territories, waters and coastal seas and other resources and to uphold their responsibilities to future generations in this regard." We recognize the need for international leaders to hold imperial nations accountable for their attacks on Indigenous lands and bodies. Locally, the continued violation of our relatives stems directly from colonial land loss policies and genocidal attacks by the US government. For as long as the settler occupation of our lands exists, our relatives will continue to bear the brunt of capitalism. Therefore, capitalism (and imperialism) must die to protect the sacred.

Recommendations

- We must end the criminalization and brutalization of water protectors and land defenders.
- We must understand that what happens to the land, happens to the people (and vice versa). The protection of relatives must include all relatives. No one is free unless we are all free.
- Public land is stolen land. Outdoor recreation is often on land that has been stolen and converted into public land. Conservationists and nature lovers who participate in progressive causes must respect the sacred, even if this means they can no longer use land for recreational activities.
- Mass movements must be willing to educate about what is sacred and why it is important to respect and protect what is sacred.
- Stolen lands must be returned. *Ba whyea* [Blue Lake] is an area which is sacred and only used by the Indigenous people of Taos Pueblo. Blue Lake was returned to Taos Pueblo in 1970, ending the termination era, which devastated Indigenous nations and caused the loss of a further 1.4 million acres of tribal land. The Blue Lake example shows how the protection of sacred sites is key to the retention, return, and restoration of stolen land.
- Greater Chaco Canyon: support people and communities directly dealing with oil and gas infrastructure; stop government-initiated lease sales for fracking operations; protest at Bureau of Land Management offices; raise concern about MMIWG2S and "man camps"; go to local organizing events and meetings to end fracking in your area.
- Mauna Kea: protest to stop the construction of the Thirty Meter Telescope; amplify the international divestment campaign; support the struggle through writing.

- Support international movements and grassroots organizing through education, solidarity events, film screenings, teach-ins, protests, and rallies.
- Provide free legal work and services for water protectors and land defenders.
- Donate to legal funds like Unist'ot'en Camp and Water Protectors Legal Collective.

Area 5: Enforcement of Treaty Rights and Other Agreements

Colonial presidents, congresses, and courts see treaties as business transactions to open up Indigenous territory for the expansion of plantation slavery, agriculture, commerce, trade, and resource extraction. It is as common for politicians to pledge to "honor the treaties" as it is for them to break or ignore treaties. To do otherwise would be contrary to the intention of invaders, which is to secure permanent white settlement by eliminating Indigenous nationhood. The colonial approach to treaties has resulted in nothing less than theft and genocide for Indigenous peoples. But it is arrogant for invaders to think their systems of diplomacy and trade are the only traditions that matter. Indigenous diplomacy proliferated before the European invasion and continues to this day.

For example, Leanne Betasamosake Simpson considers the Gdoo-naaganinaa a precolonial treaty for sharing territory between the Nishnaabeg Nation and Haudenosaunee Confederacy in what is today known as Southern Ontario. Unlike the European Westphalian state model of sovereignty—defined by exclusivity over territory—Indigenous treaties such as Gdoo-naaganinaa (which defined the shared territory as "our dish") allow for diverse, overlapping Indigenous jurisdictions and sovereignties.[8] "European political

traditions would have us believe that being sovereign means assert-ing exclusive control over a territory," the Nehiyaw scholar Emily Riddle argues, whereas Indigenous political traditions "teach us that it is through our relationship with others that we are sovereign, that sharing is not a sign of weakness but of ultimate strength and di-plomacy."[9] and diplomacy." Kul Wicasa historian Nick Estes notes that Wolakota (meaning "peace" or "treaty") originated from the Pte Sa Win, the White Buffalo Woman, who brought the Lakota Nation into correct relations with the animal and plant nations. This un-derstanding to treaty-making and diplomacy extended beyond the world of what could be considered solely *human*. Lakota people took their understanding of this original covenant with the nonhuman world with them as they entered into treaty relations with colonizing nations, like the United States. In the 1868 Fort Laramie treaty, for instance, Lakota people negotiated a thirty-two-million-acre hunt-ing territory—"so long as the buffalo may range"—in addition to a thirty-five-million-acre permanent reservation. In other words, this treaty was also to secure the future existence of the buffalo nations in relation to Lakota people, that stemmed from a covenant or treaty made by a woman—not men.[10]

These examples show that discord is resolved through creat-ing permanent political relations between parties (including oth-er-than-human nations) based on moral responsibility and good-faith pledges. The consequences for violating these Indigenous covenants extends far beyond the human world. Global warming and the sixth mass extinction event are the apocalyptic results of this cascading unbalance. While those most responsible for climate change—im-perial nations—have proposed remedies through capitalist markets and techno-fixes, none so far have sought to rectify their own irre-sponsibility. Their failure to act holds the entire future hostage.

Original instructions, which emphasize peaceful and mutual relations between humans and between humans and other-than-humans, inform the way Indigenous people have historically entered into relations with European nations. Even if original instructions are not reciprocated, each party to a treaty has equal power to interpret the meaning of the agreement. While colonizers have chosen to interpret treaties to advance their own genocidal interests, Indigenous people have never surrendered the moral authority, responsibility, or sense of justice that original instructions mandate. One of the most important expressions of this commitment is the People's Agreement signed in Cochabamba, Bolivia, which proposed not only just relations with the other-than-human world, but also upending the cause of unequal relations between entire nations and humans themselves: imperialism and capitalism.

The Indigenous Andean cosmovision of *Vivir Bien* [Living Well] and *Pachamama* [Mother Earth] are central to understanding the People's Accords. Living well is not anthropocentric, or focused solely on human relations; it is Earthcentric, focusing on the whole. It understands that capitalist domination over nature is patriarchal, and that over-consumption, which is driven by the First World, is not the solution but the problem. If all of humans consumed as much as the average US citizen, we would need four Earths to sustain it. We only have one planet to share, and just relations with the natural world are impossible without just, equitable relations among humanity first. Like the Red Deal, the People's Accords are an Indigenous treaty—a covenant—with the Earth and its people.

The US-backed, right-wing military coup that deposed MAS leader and Bolivian president Evo Morales in 2019 was also a coup against this eco-covenant and Indigenous socialism. Now, more than ever, it is necessary to reestablish correct relations by enforcing the original

covenant, a living document or treaty with the Earth. This begins by upholding the Indigenous interpretation and authority over all treaties and agreements made with colonial powers, whether these agreements were struck three hundred years ago or yesterday. There are also hundreds of multilateral agreements and treaties with social movements and the humble people of the Earth that require enforcement. We can't and won't wait for colonizers. The power is in our hands to enact natural law and restore balance in accordance with Indigenous principles.

Recommendations

- Decolonize the atmosphere. Restore to oppressed nations and developing countries the atmospheric space that is occupied by First World greenhouse gas emissions. Nations of the Global South cannot follow the same path of development of the North that require massive amounts of carbon emissions in their industrialization process. The right to develop is hindered by the colonization of the atmosphere by the First World's carbon emissions. This means the decolonization of the atmosphere through the reduction and absorption of their emissions.
- Transfer technology. First World countries must assume all the costs and technology transfer needs of oppressed nations who have lost development opportunities due to living under the boot of US imperialism or in a restricted atmospheric space.
- Open the borders. First World countries must assume all responsibility for the hundreds of millions of people that will be forced to migrate due to capitalist-driven climate change. They must eliminate their restrictive immigration policies and instead offer migrants a decent life with full human rights guarantees in their countries.

- Pay climate debt. First World countries must assume all adaptation debt related to the impacts of climate change on developing countries by providing the means to prevent, minimize, and deal with damages arising from their excessive emissions.
- Mass land return. Return land to Indigenous nations, the original caretakers. Billions of acres of territory have been taken out of Indigenous ecological stewardship, resulting in mass extinction. Restoring land to Indigenous caretakers is a necessary step towards ensuring any kind of future on this planet.
- Restore treaty-making with Indigenous nations.
- Respect and uphold Indigenous treaties as international agreements and the supreme law of the land.
- Adopt and implement the 2007 *United Nations Declaration on the Rights of Indigenous Peoples.*[11]
- Adopt and implement the 2010 People's Agreement.[12]
- Adopt and implement a plurinational governance structure, or constitution, that recognizes, upholds, and defends Indigenous sovereignty and nationhood.
- Adopt and implement the 2011 Mother Earth Accord.[13]
- Adopt and implement the Indigenous Principles of Just Transition.[14]
- Adopt and implement the 2013 Treaty to Protect the Sacred from Tar Sands Projects.[15]
- Adopt and implement the 2010 Universal Declaration of Rights of Mother Earth.[16]

Conclusion

We began *The Red Deal* with the oldest yet often forgotten struggle on this continent: ending colonial occupation. While usually erased

from the history of this nation, settler colonialism has fundamentally shaped the development of the United States and the world that it dominates economically and politically. Ending the occupation links those of us in the seat of empire with those who face its weapons, soldiers, and policies around the world. Together we share the common enemy of US imperialism. This is why we begin with ending the occupation.

The struggle against occupation on this continent has remained strong throughout history and continues (grows, even) to this day. We've seen this in the global uprisings led by Black relatives who have been resisting the colonization of Africa and the enslavement and oppression of African people stolen to work on this continent for centuries. Even with the COVID-19 pandemic, the uprisings during the summer of 2020 were some of the largest mobilizations in US history. The spread of uprisings across the country was also marked by the sharpening of tactics and clarity of the roots of the issues, with images of burned-down police precincts and flipped cop cars evoking memories of Black and Indigenous resistance to slave plantations and frontier forts. The recent calls for defunding police and prisons stretch forward from a long history of abolitionist struggle.

It is important that we continue nurturing these histories and movements of struggle against occupation on these lands and continue to build relationships with others globally who face the violence of occupation. We began in Part I with addressing those things that act as obstacles to our collective liberation: the prisons and detention centers filled with our family members; the police officers and prison guards who stand between us and the capitalist interests they defend; and the military, police, and vigilantes who murder our relatives. As we know, colonial occupation is upheld by constant threats of violence and in many instances, actual violence. It is

therefore no surprise that these obstacles to our life and well-being that employ violence in order to maintain the occupation, receive the largest proportions of resources by the US settler state. We therefore must seek to dismantle these institutions that get in our way of living good lives, so we aim to divert resources away from them through divestment.

This is just the first step. It is not enough to be *against* any one thing—even something as big, evil, and all-encompassing as colonial occupation. Ending the occupation gives us the space to breathe and envision other possibilities that we are *for*, and we must be clear about what we are for. We are for Indigenous life, for the life of all human and other-than-human beings. In order to live dignified lives, we must heal ourselves from the destruction caused by colonialism and capitalism by stopping what harms us and desecrates our land and instead begin to build what will sustain us.

CONCLUSION

Our Words are Powerful, Our Knowledge is Inevitable

Infrastructures of Relation

In 2017, Tlingit scholar Anne Spice sat down with Unist'ot'en hereditary spokesperson Freda Huson for an interview that has since appeared in *Standing with Standing Rock: Voices from the #NoDAPL Movement*, an edited volume of over forty contributors reflecting on the history and significance of the #NoDAPL uprising at Standing Rock in 2016. Spice's interview with Huson was conducted in a log cabin that Huson was asked to build in April 2010, two years after the Wet'suwet'en clans refused the British Columbia treaty process requiring them to cede their ancestral lands to Canada.

Midway through the interview, their conversation turns to the topic of critical infrastructure, a phrase that has been used repeatedly by the Canadian government to criminalize Wet'suwet'en people whose lands Canada claims to be "in the way" of lucrative oil and gas pipelines:

> Spice: I'm wondering how you think the way that industry approaches the land and the water and animals is different than the way you view those same things?

Huson: Our critical infrastructure is the clean drinking water, and the very water that the salmon spawn in. . . . That salmon is our food source, it's our main staple food. That's one of our critical infrastructures. And there's berries that are our critical infrastructure, because the berries not only feed us, they also feed the bears, and the salmon also don't just feed us, they feed the bears. . . . All of that is part of the system that our people depend on, and that whole cycle and system is our critical infrastructure, and that's what we're trying to protect, an infrastructure that we depend on.[1]

The cabin the interview was conducted in one of several structures that now make up what is commonly known as "Unist'ot'en Camp." The Unist'ot'en Camp was established "to enforce the decision to preserve the territory for future generations."[2] The cabin in which Spice and Huson are talking is built in the exact area where Trans-Canada, Enbridge, and Pacific Trails want to lay oil and gas pipelines, the critical infrastructure that Canada has waged over a decade's worth of violent evictions, demolitions, surveillance, and harassment campaigns against Wet'suwet'en people to guarantee. Still, they will not leave the camp nor abandon their territory. The Unist'ot'en, we are reminded, "are fighting for the future health of the land."[3]

In addition to defining what critical infrastructure means for the Wet'suwet'en, Huson defines what it means for settler society and corporations in Canada: "industry and government always talk about critical infrastructure, and their critical infrastructure is making money, and using destructive projects to make that money."[4] We highlight Huson's comments about critical infrastructure because they speak to the broader ethics and goals that drive the Red Deal's vision for economic and political change. As we have shown

throughout this book, a structural perspective rooted in Indigenous knowledge—particularly our traditions of science and technology—seeks to build critical infrastructures premised on methods of relationality that emphasize, above all else, caretaking and balance. This is crucial because the infrastructures we must dismantle are not only those that manifest in pipelines, bulldozers, smokestacks, concrete dams, or man camps—the material infrastructure of extractivism. Rather, the critical infrastructure we must undo is the philosophy that drives these material conditions. As Huson notes, this philosophy is money, and its primary method of relationality is destruction. There is another word for a money-driven system that expresses its existence through destruction: capitalism. Capitalism destroys life. It pollutes the rivers. It scars mountains. It starves moose, wolves, and salmon. It alienates our bonds with each other and with the Earth. Its very existence demands our disappearance.

The Red Nation is serious about building alternatives to the death world of capitalism that we currently endure. We are serious because we know what is at stake if we do not. As we say in *The Red Deal*, we have two paths: decolonization or extinction. Like the Wet'suwet'en, we are Indigenous peoples who belong to and love our nations. Our sovereignty—our very being—cannot be separated from the health and well-being of the land. Like all societies and civilizations, our relationality, and the values upon which these practices are based, is what makes us who we are. Our political orders and systems of governance only matter if we caretake the land; they are intelligible through our relationship with the land—literally.

We do not want to endure any longer; we want to thrive. It is for this reason that we cannot accept a path other than decolonization. As Sicangu Titunwan scholar Edward Valandra argues about his own nation, the Oceti Sakowin Oyate, "our sovereignty flows directly

from our origin story. . . . We must follow our original instructions: *to be a good relative*."⁵ This is precisely what our Wet'suwet'en relatives at Unist'ot'en Camp have shown us in their steadfast fight for the future health of the land. This is also what our Oceti Sakowin relatives at Standing Rock did during the #NoDAPL movement when they became water protectors to answer the call for help from their relatives of the Water Nation. "Since water is our relative, we protect all our relatives from harm," says Valandra. "Resisting DAPL was our response to a relative's call for help; answering that call was and remains our responsibility."⁶

The critical infrastructure of Indigenous worlds is, fundamentally, about responsibility and being a good relative. But our responsibilities do not happen only in the realm of political transformation. Caretaking, which we address in the introduction and in Part III, is the basis, too, for vibrant economies that must work fluidly with political structures to reinforce the world we seek to build beyond capitalism. We must thus have faith in our own forms of Indigenous political economy, the *critical infrastructures* that Huson speaks of so eloquently. We must rigorously study, theorize, enact, and experiment with these forms. While it covers ambitious terrain, *The Red Deal* at its base provides a program for study, theorization, action, and experimentation. But we must do the work. And the cold, hard truth is that we must not only be willing to do the work on a small scale whenever it suits us—in our own lives, in our families, or even in The Red Nation.

We must be willing, as our fearless Wet'suwet'en relatives have done, to *enforce* these orders on a large scale. In conversation, our The Red Nation comrade Nick Estes stated, "I don't want to just *honor* the treaties. I want to *enforce* them." We can and should implement these programs in our own communities to alleviate suffering and

protect what lands we are still able to caretake under colonial rule. To survive extinction, however, we must enforce Indigenous orders in and amongst those who have made it clear they will not stop their plunder until we are all dead. Settler and imperial nations, military superpowers, multinational corporations, and members of the ruling class are enemies of the Earth and the greatest danger to our future. How will we enforce Indigenous political, scientific, and economic orders to successfully prevent our mass ruin? This is the challenge we confront and pose in *The Red Deal*, and it is the challenge that all who take up The Red Deal must also confront.

The Power of Words

Like the phrase "land back," the Red Deal isn't entirely new. Every generation of Indigenous people since invasion has wanted land back, and so too have they wanted to restore correct relations like the ones we spell out in these pages. The aspirations for justice stem from deep-rooted traditions, practices, and knowledges embedded within the land itself. The Red Deal is a theory and a program that emerges from *experience*. It is rooted in struggle, in what we do, what we observe, and the relationships we make (and sometimes break). It is thoroughly grounded in the material world we inhabit. It does not come from thought experiments or philosophical debates. Our writing and thinking quite literally emerge from the ground up; they are always grounded in our relationship with land and with people. They are a manifestation of, and directly responsive to, action.

We have written this book not as a guidebook to help movements see what needs to be seen, or to confirm what is missing from their own struggles. It is our view that Indigenous people do not write

enough. And when we do, others rarely listen. Why else would we be on the precipice of mass extinction?

If humanity were already following the guidance of Indigenous people, we would be in a much different situation and we would not have to write yet another program for liberation. We certainly do not write enough for our own people in a way that speaks to their hardest struggles and deepest dreams. We thus take our role as revolutionaries and intellectuals seriously because we take our people seriously. We are not apart from our people; we are the people. In fact, the drafting of this text involved countless hours of meetings with Indigenous communities throughout Turtle Island and beyond. Many of the drafters are not academics or professional intellectuals in the Western sense, but nonetheless hold valuable knowledge and skills that have brought this project to fruition. The Red Deal wasn't drafted in a closed-door meeting or at the whims of a corporate-structured NGO or nonprofit. In a very Indigenous process, it was written and created through dialogue, reflection, and action.

This is a movement-document that comes from the humble people of the Earth. And we sincerely hope you find meaning in our words, that this book touches your heart and ignites your soul. Our words are sincere and our thoughts and hopes are given freely to inspire our relatives, the humble people of the Earth, to rise up and reclaim their humanity. They are, as our Diné relatives remind us, a sacred wind that carries the power to shape action.

As much as we hope *The Red Deal* inspires monumental action and mass mobilization, we also hope it inspires more writing and more thinking. Setting your pen to a piece of paper or sitting down at a computer to write a thought—let alone a book!—is, after all, action. Not to mention hard work. It is a form of what Leanne Betasamosake Simpson calls "Indigenous excellence," or rigorous

engagement with Indigenous knowledge that happens in relation to the land and to other human beings.[7] While we are also unapologetic leftists, we do not prioritize these intellectual and political traditions over Indigenous ones. If anything, we filter, center, and interpret our politics through a commitment to Indigenous political economy and futurity, first and foremost. To do otherwise would be contrary to who we are in this world.

As *The Red Deal* continues to be read, shared, debated, and implemented, we ask that its Indigenous intent and design not be decentered or whittled down for the sake of expediency, or that it be reduced to "cultural" or "spiritual" window dressing for otherwise scientific, economic-driven programs (likely designed by white dude "experts"). Unlike thinkers who center European thought, politics, and movements to not only perpetuate European colonialism but also try to apply it to the entire world, Indigenous knowledge is not parochial thought that applies to just one local culture, one place, or one time period. Indigenous knowledge is rigorous, scientific, inclusive, diverse, and ever-changing. The knowledge we share in is comprised of Indigenous science, economics, and political science that must be at the center of any climate justice program, just as our youth, women, and warriors have been since its inception.

Our emphasis on Indigenous knowledge may seem like a rehashing of what is already available to movements, worked through by other Indigenous organizations, movements, scholars, or leaders that precede us. Some may read this and feel discouraged or uninspired because we are not proposing anything new. The truth is, we are not. Not entirely, at least. The methods of decolonization and revolution we draw from, as well as our focus on how "Indigenous knowledge incites transformation and change," aren't anything new.[8] But this is because we understand the Red Deal (and The Red Nation

more broadly) as belonging to longstanding, dynamic *traditions of Indigenous resistance*. Ours is a generational fight that picks up where our predecessors and ancestors left off. We are simply attempting to fulfill those original instructions that Valandra writes about; the same instructions that our ancestors set out all those years ago to fulfill. In many ways, we hope to be the culmination of our ancestors' freedom dreams, premised always on returning to our humanity and our origins as good relatives.

What is perhaps different about the Red Deal is the scale of application we are proposing. Given the planetary reach of mass extinction caused by a global system of capitalism, our program for freedom must be equally audacious and far-reaching. There is no reason why Indigenous revolutionaries can't lead us in this collective transition to the future. There is also no excuse to continue to sideline Indigenous people or knowledge simply because of the racism and ignorance that underwrites so much of what counts for radical or revolutionary politics. The extent to which the left—particularly in North America—continues to do so will be the measure of its failure to contribute in any meaningful way to the global revolution yet to come.

The Red Nation is not asking for a seat at the table of the ruling class or of the left. It is telling humanity to listen to Indigenous people. Don't just take us seriously, take our lead, for as Haudenosaunee feminist Theresa McCarthy argues, "assertions of Indigenous knowledge" provide "models that pose alternatives to mainstream ideas," something we desperately need in these times.[9]

In her reflections on the leadership of Haudenosaunee diplomats and governance systems in the establishment of Indigenous internationalism, McCarthy reminds us that "the Haudenosaunee and other Indigenous nations of the world built an entire international

Indigenous human rights infrastructure with no resources other than words and language."[10] Our words are powerful, and our knowledge is inevitable. Both come from and reaffirm the worlds we inhabit and continue to build, even under apocalyptic conditions. They convey strength and innovation. Because we belong to long traditions of Indigenous resistance, we have done this before. As comrade Nick Estes' book states, our history is the future.[11]

In closing, we hope these words move you to act. Each day in The Red Nation we study, theorize, enact, and experiment with everything we have laid out here in *The Red Deal*. We govern ourselves and our relations according to one simple philosophy: *be a good relative*. We are, as a collective, an experiment in practicing infrastructures of Indigenous worldmaking premised on this central edict. We don't always get it right, but we refuse to give up because we carry the dreams of our ancestors in our hearts. These dreams will never steer us wrong, and they will not steer you wrong. The struggle to remember our humanity through our love for the Earth will define the future for all. Join us. We are waiting for you, we welcome you, and we are ready to act.

Appendix

Who We Are

The Red Nation is dedicated to the liberation of Native peoples from capitalism and colonialism. We center Native political agendas and struggles through direct action, advocacy, mobilization, and education. We are a coalition of Native and non-Native activists, educators, students, and community organizers advocating for Native liberation. We formed to address the marginalization and invisibility of Native struggles within mainstream social-justice organizing, and to foreground the targeted destruction of and violence towards Native life and land.

Areas of Struggle

Indigeneity: We struggle for the defense and livelihood of Native peoples and lands. Indigeneity is a political condition that challenges the existence and domination of colonial nation-states.

Liberation: We struggle for the repatriation of Native lives and land. Liberation is not about "healing" or "getting over it." It is a struggle for material and structural transformation.

Resistance: We continue the long history of Native anticolonial resistance by reviving active resistance as fundamental to liberation.

Coalition: We mobilize for widespread action and community engagement for Native struggles for liberation.

Principles of Unity

This is the Preamble to The Red Nation's Principles of Unity ratified by the first General Assembly of Freedom Councils in Albuquerque, New Mexico on August 10, 2018 (Pueblo Revolt Day). In the spirit of Popay!

We are Indigenous revolutionaries. We are comrades and relatives first and foremost. We practice radical democracy and compassion for all relatives. Despite differences in organizational role or affiliation, we are equals in struggle.

We are anticapitalist and anticolonial. We are Indigenous feminists who believe in radical relationality. We do not seek a milder form of capitalism or colonialism—we demand an entirely new system premised on peace, cooperation, and justice. For our Earth and relatives to live, capitalism and colonialism must die.

We belong to long traditions of Indigenous resistance. We claim our rightful place among all freedom fighters around the world. We are not the first, nor will we be the last. We are the ancestors from the before and the already forthcoming. By carrying this history forward, we actively create the world in which we want to live.

We seek to not just challenge power, but to build power. We are not simply a negation of the nightmarish colonial present—colonialism, capitalism, heteropatriarchy, imperialism, and white supremacy—we are the embodiment and affirmation of a coming Indigenous future, a future in which many worlds fit.

We believe that all oppressed nations have the right to self-determination—to decide their own destinies. We, The Red Nation, are self-determining peoples. We enact the principles of freedom and integrity in how we seek to live as good people of the Earth.

We organize through education and agitation for revolutionary change. We encourage our relatives and comrades to believe in revolutionary change. We advocate for global decolonization. We agitate among the poor, the working classes, the colonized, and the dispossessed to instill the confidence to fight back and take control of our destinies.

We believe in pessimism of the intellect, optimism of the will. We remain accountable to our people and our nations. We do not have "perfect" politics. We do not believe in factionalism or rigid ideology. We can die having had the "correct positions" but having accomplished nothing and freed no one. The desire to be "right" or "perfect" is the highest form of cynicism. Our role as revolutionaries is to cheerlead the movement at all turns. Above all else, we desire to be free and believe we will win. Optimism will thrive so long as we struggle for freedom.

We believe in correct ideas, which only come through revolutionary praxis and struggle. Our power and judgment comes from the labor of our struggle.

We are not "above" the people. When the people move, we move with them. We are the "permanent persuaders" who believe revolutionary change is not only possible but inevitable. Like our hearts, our politics are down and to the left. And because we are the "five-fingered ones," our fists are the size of our hearts. We raise our fists to lift the hearts of our people. We give everything and take nothing for ourselves.

We uphold personal and organizational integrity at all turns of the movement. Change is dialectical and full of contradictions. It often

comes without notice or without being noticed. Reactionary tendencies and contradictions will seek to destroy our momentum, diminish our optimism, and test our integrity. They will come in many, and oftentimes unexpected, forms. Even when in doubt, we pledge to remain faithful to our political principles and steadfast in our commitment to revolutionary struggle and optimism.

We are The Red Nation.

Notes

Introduction

1   Elodie Descamps and Tarik Bouafia, "In Moments of Crisis, Behind Every Moderate Liberal, There's a Fascist: An Interview with Álvaro García Linera," trans. David Broder, *Jacobin*, November 20, 2019, https://www.jacobinmag.com/2019/11/alvaro-garcia-linera-bolivia-coup-evo-morales-mas.

2   Org4justice, "#LANDBACK Update from Gidimt'en Territory" (video), January 18, 2020, https://www.youtube.com/watch?v=hUza4Bdcyfo&list=PLgW3qVAvzOI55XNUMw-qg6xf66MD5RkQu&index=4.

3   Vine Deloria Jr., "This Country Was a Lot Better Off When the Indians Were Running It," *The New York Times*, March 8, 1970, https://www.nytimes.com/1970/03/08/archives/this-country-was-a-lot-better-off-when-the-indians-were-running-it.html.

4   Malcolm Harris, "Indigenous Knowledge Has Been Warning Us About Climate Change for Centuries," *Pacific Standard*, March 4, 2019, https://psmag.com/ideas/indigenous-knowledge-has-been-warning-us-about-climate-change-for-centuries.

5   Tim Giago, "Hugo Chaves Steps Up for Native Americans and the Poor," *HuffPost*, March 3, 2007 [updated May 25, 2011], https://www.huffpost.com/entry/hugo-chavez-steps-up-for-_b_43630.

6   Winona LaDuke, "Native American Activist Winona LaDuke at Standing Rock: It's Time to Move On From Fossil Fuels," interview by Amy Goodman, *Democracy Now*, September 12, 2016, https://www.democracynow.org/2016/9/12/native_american_activist_winona_laduke_at.

7   Lee Schlenker, "The War on Cuba and Venezuela," *Counter Punch*, October 19, 2020, https://www.counterpunch.org/2020/10/19/the-war-on-cuba-and-venezuela/.

8   Daniel Dickinson, "COVID-19: UN chief calls for global ceasefire to focus on 'the true fight for our lives,'" *UN News*, March 23, 2020, https://news.un.org/en/story/2020/03/1059972.

9   Johanna Bozuwa and Thomas M. Hanna, "Democratize Finance, Euthanize the Fossil Fuel Industry," *Jacobin*, March 3, 2019, https://jacobinmag.com/2019/03/green-new-deal-financing-fossil-fuels.

10 "Talking Points on The AOC-Markey Green New Deal (GND) Resolution," Indigenous Environmental Network, n.d., https://www.ienearth.
org/talking-points-on-the-aoc-markey-green-new-deal-gnd-resolution/.

11 "Keep In the Ground News Archives," Indigenous Environmental Network, https://www.ienearth.org/keepitintheground/.

12 Alleen Brown, "Pipeline Opponents Strike Back Against Anti-Protest
Laws: Two Lawsuits in Louisiana and South Dakota are the First Signs
of Resistance to Efforts by the Fossil Fuel Industry to Criminalize
Pipeline Protests," *The Intercept*, March 23, 2019, https://theintercept.
com/2019/05/23/pipeline-protest-laws-louisiana-south-dakota/.

13 "Nature's Dangerous Decline 'Unprecedented' Species Extinction Rates
'Accelerating,'" UN Environment Programme, May 6, 2019, https://www.
unenvironment.org/news-and-stories/press-release/natures-danger-
ous-decline-unprecedented-species-extinction-rates.

14 "Indigenous Peoples," The World Bank, https://www.worldbank.org/en/
topic/indigenouspeoples.

15 Alleen Brown, "Trump Administration Asks Congress to Make Disrupting Pipeline Construction a Crime Punishable by 20 Years In Prison,"
The Intercept, June 5, 2019, https://theintercept.com/2019/06/05/pipe-
line-protests-proposed-legislation-phmsa-alec/.

16 Senate Committee on Apropriations, "National Security Implications of
Climate-Related Risks and a Changing Climate," Congressional Report,
July 23, 2015, https://archive.defense.gov/pubs/150724-congressional-re-
port-on-national-implications-of-climate-change.pdf.

17 Daniel R. Coats, "Statement for the Record: Worldwide Threat Assessment of the US Intelligence Community," Office of the Director of
National Intelligence, January 29, 2019, https://www.odni.gov/index.php/
newsroom/congressional-testimonies/item/1947-statement-for-the-re-
cord-worldwide-threat-assessment-of-the-us-intelligence-community.

18 Juliet Eilperin, Josh Dawsey, and Brady Dennis, "White House blocked
intelligence agency's written testimony calling climate change 'possibly
catastrophic,'" *The Washington Post*, June 8, 2019, https://www.washing-
tonpost.com/climate-environment/2019/06/08/white-house-blocked-in-
telligence-aides-written-testimony-saying-human-caused-cli-
mate-change-could-be-possibly-catastrophic/

19 Jill Stein and Howie Hawkins, "The Green New Deal," Green Party US, https://www.gp.org/green_new_deal.

20 Deloria, "This Country Was a Lot Better Off."

Part I: Divest: End the Occupation

1 Roxanne Dunbar-Ortiz, *An Indigenous Peoples' History of the United States* (Boston: Beacon Press, 2014), 7.

2 United Nations General Assembly, "Convention on the Prevention and Punishment of the Crime of Genocide," 260 (III) A (Paris, December 9, 1948), https://www.un.org/en/genocideprevention/genocide-convention.shtml.

3 Oliphant v. Suquamish Indian Tribe, 435 U.S. 191 (1978), https://supreme.justia.com/cases/federal/us/435/191/#201.

4 Andrew Curley, "Beyond Environmentalism: #NoDAPL as Assertion of Tribal Sovereingty," in *Standing with Standing Rock: Voices from the #NoDAPL Movement*, ed. Nick Estes and Jaskiran Dhillon (Minneapolis: University of Minnesota, 2019), 161.

5 Scorched earth campaigns were one of the weapons used by European colonial settlers and US military forces in their wars against Indigenous people; i.e., the destruction of villages, food stores, crops, livestock, and wildlife were used to undermine Indigenous resistance to colonization.

6 Elizabeth Cook-Lynn, *New Indians, Old Wars* (Chicago: University of Illinois Press, 2007), 72.

7 Cook-Lynn, *New Indians*, 71.

8 Cook-Lynn, *New Indians*, 72.

9 Global Alliance for the Rights of Nature, "People's Conference on Climate Change and the Rights of Mother Earth" (Cochabamba, Bolivia, April 2010), https://therightsofnature.org/cochabama-rights/?cli_action=1604285273.892.

10 United Nations General Assembly, *Universal Declaration of Human Rights*, 217 (III) A (Paris, December 10, 1948), https://www.un.org/en/universal-declaration-human-rights/.

11 Arab Resource and Organization Center, "Statement on Supreme Court's Partial Reinstatement of Muslim Travel Ban," July 29, 2017, http://arabor-ganizing.org/freedom-to-stay-freedom-to-move-freedom-to-return-free-dom-to-resist/.

Part II: Heal Our Bodies: Reinvest In Our Common Humanity

1   H. Damon Matthews, "Quantifying Historical Carbon and Climate Debts Among Nations," *Nature Climate Change* 6 (2016): 60–64.

2   Nancy Pindus et al., *Housing Needs of American Indians and Alaska Natives in Tribal Areas: A Report From the Assessment of American Indian, Alaska Native, and Native Hawaiian Housing Needs* [Executive Summary] (Washington, DC: U.S. Department of Housing and Urban Development, January 2017), https://www.huduser.gov/portal/sites/default/files/pdf/HousingNeedsAmerIndians-ExecSumm.pdf.

3   Alexia Fernández Campbell, "Gas Leaks, Mold, and Rats: Millions of Americans Live in Hazardous Homes," *The Atlantic*, July 25, 2016, https://www.theatlantic.com/business/archive/2016/07/gas-leaks-mold-and-rats-millions-of-americans-live-in-hazardous-homes/492689/.

4   Centers for Disease Control and Prevention, "Lesbian, Gay, Bisexual, and Transgender Health," https://www.cdc.gov/lgbthealth/youth.htm.

5   Helen Oliff, "Graduation Rates & American Indian Education, Partnership with Native Americans, May 16, 2017, http://blog.nativepartnership.org/graduation-rates-american-indian-education/.

6   Edward R. Burchick, Jessica C. Barnett, and Rachel D. Upton, *Health Insurance Coverage in the United States: 2018* (Washington, DC: United States Census Bureau, November 8, 2019), http://www.census.gov/content/dam/Census/library/publications/2019/demo/p60-267.pdf.

7   Patrick Varine, "Auditor General: Billions in Transportation Funding Diverted to Pennsylvania State Police," *TribLive*, April 25, 2019, https://triblive.com/news/pennsylvania/auditor-general-billions-in-transportation-funding-diverted-to-pennsylvania-state-police/.

8   Adie Tomer, *Transit Access and Zero-Vehicle Households*, Metropolitian Policy Program at Brooklings, (Washington, DC: Brookings, 2011), https://www.brookings.edu/wp-content/uploads/2016/06/0818_transportation_tomer.pdf.

9   Nathaniel J. Pollock et al.," Global Incidence of Suicide Among Indige-
    nous peoples: A Systemic Review," *BMC Medicine* 16(1), August 20, 2018,
    https://bmcmedicine.biomedcentral.com/articles/10.1186/s12916-018-
    1115-6.

10 Centers for Disease Control and Prevention, *Morbidity and Morality Report*
    65(9), August 2016, https://www.cdc.gov/mmwr/volumes/65/ss/pdfs/
    ss6509.pdf.

11 Sandy E. James et al., *Executive Summary of the Report of the 2015 U.S.
    Transgender Survey* (Washington, DC: National Center for Transgender
    Equality, December 2016), https://transequality.org/sites/default/files/
    docs/usts/USTS-Executive-Summary-Dec17.pdf.

12 "Fast Facts: Native American Youth and Indian Country," Center for
    Native American Youth, https://www.cnay.org/resource-hub/fast-facts/.

13 U.S. Department of Agriculture, "Current Population Survey Food Secu-
    rity Supplement," December 2019, https://www.ers.usda.gov/data-prod-
    ucts/food-security-in-the-united-states/

14 U.S. Department of Agriculture, "Food Waste FAQs," https://www.usda.
    gov/foodwaste/faqs.

15 Phillip Kaufman, Chris Dicken, and Ryan Williams, *Measuring Access to
    Healthful, Affordable Food in American Indian and Alaska Native Tribal Ar-
    eas* (Washington, DC: U.S. Department of Agriculture, December 2014),
    https://www.ers.usda.gov/webdocs/publications/43905/49690_eib131_er-
    rata.pdf?v=0.

16 U.S. Department of Agriculture, *Measuring Access*, https://www.ers.usda.
    gov/amber-waves/2013/march/different-measures-of-food-access-in-
    form-different-solutions.

17 Devon A. Mihesuah and Elizabeth Hoover, eds., *Indigenous Food Sover-
    eignty in the United States: Restoring Cultural Knowledge, Protecting Envi-
    ronments, and Regaining Health*. Norman, OK: University of Oklahoma
    Press, 2019.

18 United Nations Office on Drugs and Crime (UNODC), *Global Study
    on Homicide: Gender-Related Killing of Women and Girls* (Vienna, 2018),
    http://www.unodc.org/documents/data-and-analysis/GSH2018/GSH18_
    Gender-related_killing_of_women_and_girls.pdf.

19 "Ending Violence Against Native Women," Indian Law Resource Center, November 2, 2020, https://indianlaw.org/issue/ending-violence-against-native-women.

20 André B. Rosay, "Violence Against American Indian and Alaska Native Women and Men: 2010 Findings From the National Intimate Partner and Sexual Violence Survey," *National Institute of Justice Research Report* (Washington, DC: U.S. Department of Justice, May 2016), https://www.ncjrs.gov/pdffiles1/nij/249736.pdf.

21 Rosay, "Violence Against American Indian and Alaska Native Women and Men."

22 National Center for Transgender Equality, *2015 U.S. Transgender Survey*, December 2016, https://transequality.org/sites/default/files/docs/usts/USTS-Executive-Summary-Dec17.pdf.

23 Urban Indian Health Institute, "Our Bodies, Our Stories: Our work to advocate and provide data to protect Native women and girls," https://www.uihi.org/projects/our-bodies-our-stories/.

24 Andrew Burmon, "Police, Domestic Violence, and Home: Cops Abuse Wives and Kids at Staggering Rates," *Fatherly*, November 20, 2020, https://www.fatherly.com/love-money/police-brutality-and-domestic-violence/.

Part III: Heal Our Planet: Reinvest In Our Common Future

1 Kanahus Manuel and Naomi Klein, "'Land Back' is more than a slogan for a resurgent Indigenous movement," *The Globe and Mail*, November 19, 2020, https://www.theglobeandmail.com/opinion/article-land-back-is-more-than-a-slogan-for-a-resurgent-indigenous-movement/.

2 Vijay Prashad, "After Morales Ousted in Coup, the Lithium Question Looms Large in Bolivia," *Common Dreams*, November 12, 2019, https://www.commondreams.org/views/2019/11/12/after-morales-ousted-coup-lithium-question-looms-large-bolivia.

3 Gerald Clarke, "Bringing the Past to the Present: Traditional Indigenous Farming in Southern California," in *Indigenous Food Sovereignty in the United States: Restoring Cultural Knowledge, Protecting Environments, and Regaining Health*, ed. Devon Mihesuah and Elizabeth Hoover (Norman, OK: University of Oklahoma Press, 2019), 253–275.

4   Devon Mihesuah and Elizabeth Hoover, "Introduction," *Indigenous Food Sovereignty in the United States*, 3–25.

5   Michelle Sarche and Paul Spicer, "Poverty and Health Disparities for American Indian and Alaska Native Children: Current Knowledge and Future Prospects," *Annals of the New York Academy of Sciences*, Vol. 1136(1), 2008): 126–136.

6   Traditional Native American Farmers Association (TNAFA) and the New Mexico Acequia Association (NMAA), "A Declaration of Seed Sovereignty: A Living Document for New Mexico" (New Mexico, March 11, 2006), www.tnafa.org/declaration-seed-sovereignty.html.

7   Parliamentary Counsel Office of New Zealand and New Zealand Ministry of Justice, *Te Awa Tupua (Whanganui River Claims Settlement) Act 2017*, Public Act No. 7 (New Zealand, March 20, 2017), http://www.legislation.govt.nz/act/public/2017/0007/latest/whole.html.

8   See Leanne Simpson, "Looking after Gdoo-naaganinaa: Precolonial Nishnaabeg Diplomatic and Treaty Relationships," *Wicazo Sa Review* 23(2), January 2008: 29–42.

9   Emily Riddle, "mâmawiwikowin: Shared First Nations and Métis Jurisdiction on the Prairies *Briarpatch*, September 10, 2020, https://briarpatchmagazine.com/articles/view/mamawiwikowin.

10 Nick Estes, *Our History Is the Future: Standing Rock Versus the Dakota Access Pipeline, and the Long Tradition of Indigenous Resistance* (New York: Verso, 2019), 109–110.

11 United Nations, *United Nations Declaration on the Rights of Indigenous Peoples*, Resolution 61/295, September 13, 2007, https://www.un.org/esa/socdev/unpfii/documents/DRIPS_en.pdf.

12 "People's Agreement," World People's Conference on Climate Change and the Rights of Mother Earth (Cochabamba, Bolivia, April 22, 2010), https://pwccc.wordpress.com/2010/04/24/peoples-agreement/.

13 "Mother Earth Accord," Indigenous Environmental Network, September 15, 2011, https://www.ienearth.org/motherearth-accord/.

14 Indigenous Environmental Network, "Indigenous Principles of Just Transition: Responsibility and Relationship, Sovereignty, Transformation for Action, August 2018, https://www.ienearth.org/wp-content/uploads/2018/08/PrinciplesJustTransition-BW.pdf.

15   Indigenous Environmental Network, *International Treaty to Protect the Sacred from Tar Sands Projects*, January 25, 2013, https://www.ienearth.org/international-treaty-to-protect-the-sacred-from-tar-sands-projects/.

16   "Universal Declaration of the Rights of Mother Earth,", World People's Conference on Climate Change and the Rights of Mother Earth, (Cochabamba, Bolivia, April 22, 2010), https://therightsofnature.org/universal-declaration/.

Conclusion: Our Words are Powerful, Our Knowledge is Inevitable

1   Anne Spice, "Heal the People, Heal the Land: An Interview with Freda Huson," in *Standing with Standing Rock: Voices from the #NoDAPL Movement*, ed. Nick Estes and Jaskiran Dhillon (Minneapolis: University of Minnesota, 2019), 210–221, 215.

2   Unist'ot'en, "Background of the Campaign," https://unistoten.camp/no-pipelines/background-of-the-campaign/.

3   Unist'ot'en, "Background of the Campaign."

4   Spice, "Heal the People, Heal the Land," 215.

5   Edward Valandra, "Mni Wiconi: Water is [More Than] Life," in *Standing with Standing Rock: Voices from the #NoDAPL Movement*, ed. Nick Estes and Jaskiran Dhillon (Minneapolis: University of Minnesota, 2019), 71–89, 73.

6   Valandra, "Mni Wiconi."

7   Leanne Betasamosake Simpson, *As We Have Always Done: Indigenous Freedom Through Radical Resistance* (Minneapolis: University of Minnesota Press, 2017).

8   Theresa McCarthy, *In Divided Unity: Haudenosaunee Reclamation at Grand River* (Tucson: University of Arizona Press, 2016), 8.

9   McCarthy, *In Divided Unity*, 10.

10   McCarthy, *In Divided Unity*, 11.

11   Estes, *Our History Is the Future.*

RED MEDIA

About Red Media Series

Red Media was a movement before it was a media project. The idea arose on the heels of an anti-police violence movement in Tiwa Territory (Albuquerque, NM) and after brutal slayings of Indigenous people by settler vigilantes. A revolutionary, Indigenous-led organization—The Red Nation—was formed to correct these injustices.

What we learned from our work in The Red Nation is that there are few venues for Indigenous writing—let alone writing that centers Indigenous intelligence in all its forms. Red Media is our response to this need: a press and media project run entirely for and by Indigenous people. We produce writing and work according to our own intellectual traditions, not those imposed upon us by settler culture. We believe in Indigenous abundance and aim to inspire, caretake, and hold space for Indigenous writers by providing them a platform they may not otherwise have.

Red Media publishes a wide range of work including: poetry, photography, Indigenous botany, academic publications, land as pedagogy, memoir, manifestos, journalism, children's books, Indigenous language resources, history, politics, resource manuals, biographies, fiction, creative writing, edited collections, and much more.

Our mission is to nourish, sustain, and build Indigenous movements that not only protect life on a planet on the verge of ecological collapse but also provide models for a future premised on justice. The stakes are clear: it's decolonization or extinction.

About Common Notions

Common Notions is a publishing house and programming platform that advances new formulations of liberation and living autonomy. Our books provide timely reflections, clear critiques, and inspiring strategies that amplify movements for social justice.

By any media necessary, we seek to nourish the imagination and generalize common notions about the creation of other worlds beyond state and capital. Our publications trace a constellation of critical and visionary meditations on the organization of freedom. Inspired by various traditions of autonomism and liberation—in the United States and internationally, historically and emerging from contemporary movements—our publications provide resources for a collective reading of struggles past, present, and to come.

Common Notions regularly collaborates with editorial houses, political collectives, militant authors, and visionary designers around the world. Our political and aesthetic interventions are dreamt and realized in collaboration with Antumbra Designs.

commonnotions.org / info@commonnotions.org

Become a Monthly Sustainer

These are decisive times, ripe with challenges and possibility, heartache and beautiful inspiration. More than ever, we are in need of timely reflections, clear critiques, and inspiring strategies that can help movements for social justice grow and transform society. Help us amplify those necessary words, deeds, and dreams that our liberation movements and our worlds so need.

Movements are sustained by people like you, whose fugitive words, deeds, and dreams bend against the world of domination and exploitation.

For collective imagination, dedicated practices of love and study, and organized acts of freedom.

By any media necessary. With your love and support.

Monthly sustainers start at $12 and $25.

Join us at commonnotions.org/sustain.

More from Common Notions

Hope Against Hope:
Writings on Ecological Crisis

Out of the Woods Collective

978-1-942173-20-5
$20.00
272 pages

In *Hope Against Hope*, the Out of the Woods Collective investigates the critical relation between climate change and capitalism and calls for the expansion of our conceptual toolbox to organize within and against ecological crisis characterized by deepening inequality, rising far-right movements, and—relatedly—more frequent and devastating disasters. While much of environmentalist and leftist discourse in this political moment remain oriented toward horizons that repeat and renew racist, anti-migrant, nationalist, and capitalist assumptions, Out of the Woods charts a revolutionary course adequate to our times.

At the center of the renewed political orientation *Hope Against Hope* expounds is an abolitionist approach to border imperialism, reactionary ecology, and state violence that underpins many green solutions and modes of understanding nature. Their stunning conclusion to the disarray of politics in our seemingly end times is the urgency of creating what Out of the Woods calls "disaster communism"—the collective power to transform our future political horizons from the ruins and establish a climate future based in common life.

More from Common Notions

Abolishing Carceral Society

Abolition Collective

978-1-942173-08-3
$20.00
256 pages

In the first of a series of publications, the Abolition Collective renews and boldly extends the tradition of "abolition-democracy" espoused by figures like W.E.B. Du Bois, Angela Davis, and Joel Olson. Through study and publishing, the Abolition Collective supports radical scholarly and activist research, recognizing that the most transformative scholarship is happening both in the movements themselves and in the communities with whom they organize.

Through essays, interviews, visual art, and poetry, each presented in an accessible manner, the work engages with the meaning, practices, and politics of abolitionism in a range of historical and geographical contexts, including: prison and police abolitionism, border abolition, decolonization, slavery abolitionism, antistatism, antiracism, labor organizing, anticapitalism, radical feminism, queer and trans politics, Indigenous people's politics, sex worker organizing, migrant activism, social ecology, animal rights and liberation, and radical pedagogy.

More from Common Notions

Making Abolitionist Worlds

Abolition Collective

978-1-942173-17-5
$20.00
272 pages

What does an abolitionist world look like? Insights from today's international abolitionist movement reveal a world to win.

Making Abolitionist Worlds gathers key insights and interventions from today's international abolitionist movement to pose the question: what does an abolitionist world look like? The Abolition Collective investigates the core challenges to social justice and the liberatory potential of social movements today from a range of personal, political, and analytical points of view, underscoring the urgency of an abolitionist politics that places prisons and policing at the center of its critique and actions.

Centering and amplifying the continual struggles of incarcerated people who are actively working to transform prisons from the inside, *Making Abolitionist Worlds* animates the idea of abolitionist democracy and demands a radical re-imagining of the meaning and practice of freedom.

More from Common Notions

For Health Autonomy:
Horizons of Care Beyond Autonomy—
Reflections From Greece

CareNotes Collective

978-1-942173-14-4
$15.00
144 pages

The present way of life is a war against our bodies. Nearly everywhere, we are caught in a crumbling health system that furthers our misery and subordination to the structural violence of capital and a state that only intensifies our general precarity. Can we build the capacity and necessary infrastructure to heal ourselves and transform the societal conditions that continue to mentally and physically harm us?

Amidst the perpetual crises of capitalism is a careful resistance—organized by medical professionals and community members, students and workers, citizens and migrants. *For Health Autonomy* explores the landscape of care spaces coordinated by autonomous collectives in Greece. These projects operate in fierce resistance to austerity, state violence and abandonment, and the neoliberal structure of the healthcare industry that are failing people.

For Health Autonomy is a powerful collection of first-hand accounts of those who join together to build new possibilities of care and develop concrete alternatives based on the collective ability of communities and care workers to replace our dependency on police and prisons.